One Without The Other

AN AUTOBIOGRAPHY OF GRIEF AND INTUITION

By Toni Geving

One Without The Other

AN AUTOBIOGRAPHY OF GRIEF AND INTUITION

Written By Toni Geving

Edited by Julie Pritschet

ISBN: 978-0-9983961-0-1

Published by:

Being Whole Press

Minnesota

Dedication

I dedicate this book to all of the souls that have passed from this realm to the next and helped me understand that there is something after this life on earth.

To my John, who made the choice to leave so that I could become the person I was meant to be. You recognized your inability to expand with me and chose to help me from the other side.

To my father, who persisted in presenting his spirit, so that I would remember him through my gift of sight. I am sure that you passed part of my gift to me.

To Callifina, I am forever grateful for your silliness and your appreciation for nonsense. I will always remember your lovely spirit and many Cally-isms- e-er-lala, monkey doodle donkey, platypottomuses, and a caca tutu.

Acknowledgements

I want to thank my whole tribe, who extend beyond the limits of blood relationships and conventional definitions of family. Through everything that has happened, you have been loving and supportive of me, even if you questioned my gifts. I want you to know how appreciated you are and how grateful I am to be experiencing this life with you as my friends and family.

To my mother, who thought it was "wonderful" that I saw spirit and encouraged me to be honest and take responsibility for my actions when I was acting like a delinquent. You knew my gifts from the beginning and understood that my fear of them made me act less than honorable. Thank you for always loving me anyway.

I owe much love, gratitude and respect to Chris, who helped me evolve while she was dealing with her own evolution through cancer.

Thank you to my partners in business, Eva and Claire Marie, who encouraged me and inspired me with their own practice, then trusted me to be a part of what they had created.

Thank you to Julie for looking at this with fresh eyes. I still think "dammit" should be spelled "damnit". But, who am I to argue with the majority?

Introduction

In the past seven years, I have been on an incredible path of discovery. Not everyone would describe their challenges in this way, but I have found it to be true. Every twist and turn in my road has yielded lessons, as did the individuals that played parts in my story. At some point, I chose to learn from every experience I had with every person that touched my life.

As I started to incorporate what I know as intuition into my business, my clients asked for more information. When I began doing group readings and parties for people, I had to introduce myself and how I received information. These groups always had a healthy mix of believers, skeptics, curious and reserved attendees. Yet, more often than not, I was asked more questions about my gifts and how they came to me. At some point, I realized that it was not my job to make the skeptic a believer in my work. It was my job to give them what spirit thought they needed to know and to work with integrity.

When I told one of my brothers that I saw dead people and angels, he reacted from his own disbelief in an afterlife. He told me not to tell anyone. It was already too late. I had been offering readings to my clients for two years. "I don't believe in that. When you die, you die. There is nothing after death." I did not believe it was my job to convince him otherwise. He went to Catholic Catechism just as I did. Plus, his experiences were different than mine. Regardless of whether or not he was a believer in God, or life after death, he was a good person who cared about me and did many things to show me he cared.

Believe me when I tell you, I did not write this book to make you believe in mediums, psychics, or paranormal science. I wrote this book because I had suffered trauma-through physical injury and the deaths of a spouse and best friend. Even in my suffering, I recognized the gifts of those events. I wrote this book so others could maybe understand that there are gifts in the bad stuff that happens. But, mostly, I wrote this book because I needed to tell this part of my story.

Further, I have to explain that this was a new beginning for me. Everything I wrote is the truth as I remember it. Many parts of the story have been told to clients and friends, who told me that I should write a book. There are a couple parts that may be out of order. However, they did happen. With respect to everyone having a right to their own version of the truth, this book was my truth. I present it with love and only good intentions.

I hope you enjoy this first part of my story.

Toni Geving
June 29, 2016
Minnesota

Chapter 1

What Day Is It?

The sub-zero temperatures of January in Western Wisconsin would detour anyone from walking on ice-covered sidewalks in the pursuit of upholding a New Year's resolution. Even I questioned the sanity of my actions, as I started out on my walk, bundled up in layers and a fleece headband. What was my resolution anyway? Did I have one? Yes! I did. Mine was to really lose weight and live a healthier life in 2009. So, it was this that started me walking on that day, the first of January, 2009 at 3:30 in the afternoon.

As I was walking, I started thinking about our New Year's resolutions we had made as a couple. My husband and I had made several resolutions in the nine New Year's we'd been together. However, he was not having any of it in 2009, our tenth year together. After a year of him hiding his chew in his boot and lying about it to me, I decided I did not want to be responsible for him doing something he didn't want to do. I had nagged him so much about taking care of himself that it was exhausting thinking that I was somehow responsible for him. But, then, maybe when I got married, I took on the responsibility of protecting more than his heart? His resistance of quitting the nasty habit of chewing on tobacco made me mad. Yet, his resistance to going to the doctor and getting a regular physical just irritated me.

About a mile from the house, I was starting to think that it would be dark before I got back. I knew that he was home watching football and would not be thinking about dinner. He wouldn't even be worried about me. It wasn't that he didn't love me. It was that he just didn't worry. Or, he did not show that he worried. That was one of the things I loved about him. But, it was exactly opposite of me. I worried about everything. When I was going into a full-blown anxiety attack about our financial predicament, he just rolled over it. "You cannot do anything more than you are doing. Everything will work out."

I was just contemplating how quickly I could walk the mile home, when I noticed a guy blowing snow from a driveway next to the sidewalk on which I was walking. I slipped and fell to my knees. Waving at the man as I stood up, I laughed at my own clumsiness. I don't know how many steps I took, or what exactly happened. Yet, I remember thinking, "Meadowlark Lane. That's where Kim and Dave live."

First, I became aware of my breath, as I inhaled the icy air into my lungs. It filled me with awareness. Then, it filled me with pain in my head, neck and shoulders. What came next was the realization that my head was on ice and seemed to be stuck to it, briefly. My eyes were looking up at the sky, clouds, and two- maybe four- faces. Or, was I seeing double? When did the clouds move in? And, who are these people? Why am I lying down... outside?

As I sat up, the world spun around me. The woman, that seemed to appear while I was sprawled out on the sidewalk, told me to "just sit there a minute." I did, because I realized that I was seeing two of her. I got to my knees and knelt on the icy, snow-covered sidewalk. I assured these strangers that had come to my aid that I believed I was fine, just needed to sit still a minute. I could feel the cold air on my head and I took my glove off to feel the back of my head. It hurt and was wet and sticky. The woman looked where I was touching and made a face while saying, "Ooo! You are bleeding."

It was the weirdest thing. I don't remember her going anywhere. All of a sudden, she was giving me a paper towel to press against the back of my head. She asked if she should call an ambulance. I said, "No. I will just call my husband," as I took my cell phone out of my pocket and selected my "Fave 5" icon, which noted the word "Home" on it. At this point, I had already realized that I could not move my head without feeling like my whole body was spinning in rapid circles. Then, I felt as if I would vomit.

My husband answered the phone, "Hello?"

"John?" I asked, as if I was guessing at his name.

"Yes?"

"Can you come get me?"

"What?" he asked.

"Can you come get me?"

"Um," he hesitated. Then, went on to say, "Wouldn't that defeat the purpose of you going out there in the first place?"

"I am bleeding from my head and everything is spinning. I don't think I can make it back walking," I explained.

"What?" he asked in disbelief. "Where are you?"

"Um...where am I?" I asked him, as if he knew.

I looked at the lady next to me and she must have seen the confusion on my face because she provided the answer. "Bilmar."

"I am on Bilmar," I explained, looking up at the street sign, "and Meadowlark."

"Oh, all right, I will be there in a couple minutes!" he told me.

"OK, bye!" I hung up. I said that he was coming to get me and that I was fine. I never thought to get their names, or the address of the house where I fell. I never thought that I would need it. Of course, my only thoughts were about my headache, dizziness and pain in my shoulder and neck. I tried to stand up straight while waiting for John, realizing it was a really bad idea. The woman grabbed me and told me to sit down. Of course, I tried to ignore her and stood- hoping the world would stop spinning around me. Immediately, I sat back down on the sidewalk because the snowbanks were too high.

Sitting on the sidewalk, I looked at the ice where I slipped. Now frozen, my blood stained it. In addition, a cold wind seemed to be clotting the blood on my head, too. As I sat there, my thoughts jumped around like a grasshopper. "Was that my blood? How long have I been here? What day is it? When is John going to get here? What time is it? Why am I cold? Why am I here? Where was I going? What day is it? God, my head hurts. It's cold out here. Why am I sitting on a sidewalk? Oh, that's right! My head hurts and it's bleeding. Who are these people? What day is it?" To be honest, I don't know that I was not asking these questions aloud. The woman was looking at me like I had two heads. Maybe I did have two heads? She did, sometimes. Then, she would morph into one head.

It was getting dark. "Did I call John?" I wondered. "How long ago did I call him? Was he at work? Wait! What day is it?" I remember thinking that he took a long time coming for me. The woman stayed with me. The man went back to blowing snow. But, the noise was hurting my head.

There was so much noise at that moment. I wanted it to be quiet, but there was so much chatter. I couldn't concentrate.

I wondered if it was the woman that was talking to me. When I looked at her and asked her what she had said, she stated that she had not said anything. Then, she asked me if I was sure I was all right. Maybe I had been talking out loud? "I'm fine," I told her. Yet, I was starting to wonder how long it had been since I called my husband. It seemed like I had been sitting on the sidewalk for an hour. It was getting dark. I was getting colder and more panicked sitting there. I hurt everywhere. What was I doing waiting on a sidewalk?

When I set out on my walk, the sun was out. For some reason, I knew that there was a difference in the light when I opened my eyes on the sidewalk. There was no sun shining when I opened my eyes. While I waited for John, I tried to make sense of my rapid thoughts and the whispers I was hearing. Voices, light, and confusion would come into my head and fade away, as if someone was playing with the volume control in my ears. Yet, the woman on the sidewalk was not talking to me and I don't think I was talking to her.

I have no idea how long it took for John to get to me. The concept of time eluded me at the moment. When I saw the round lights of a white Jeep Wrangler with a tan hard top coming down the road, I felt relief to finally see something and someone familiar. The woman helped me stand up and the spinning started again. I must have looked like I needed his help, as John stopped and got out of the vehicle to help me get into it. Stepping up onto the runner step and into the Jeep almost sent me sprawling again. He put on my seatbelt because I could not figure out how to do it.

After the car door shut and John started driving, I asked, "What day is it?"

"Thursday," he said with a laugh.

"Were you at work?"

"Nooo?" he drew out.

"What took you so long?" I asked. I was irritated because my head was pounding and spinning. "What day is it?"

"It is New Year's day, Toni. We don't have to work," he explained.

"Shit!" I exclaimed. "Did I miss Christmas?"

"No." He was now looking at me with a combination of amusement and concern. I could tell he was going to start laughing. "What happened?"

"I'm bleeding," I said, as if that was enough of an explanation. "What day is it?"

"I told you, it is January 1st- New Year's Day."

"I missed Christmas?" I could not remember what I did for Christmas, but I remembered it came before New Year's. "Can you turn off the radio?"

"You did not miss Christmas," he said, with a laugh this time. "The radio is not on."

I was getting frustrated with him and my head was pounding. "Well, what is that noise?"

"What noise?"

We had driven only a couple blocks by this time. "What day is it John?"

"It's January first, two thousand nine." I don't think he laughed this time, but he answered patiently.

"Did I miss Christmas?'

"No, Dear. We went to your Mom's Saturday. Don't you remember?"

"No. How come I don't remember?"

"I think you hit your head pretty hard. We better go to the ER."

"No," I assured him, "I'm fine."

He sighed, knowing that I wasn't fine. He raised his hand with two fingers, then three, switching them back and forth. "Tell me, how many fingers am I holding up?" It was an old joke he used to pull with his daughter. It made me dizzy.

"I don't know. You're making me dizzy."

In the mile drive home, I repeatedly asked him what day it was. He patiently answered it every time. He assured me that I did not miss Christmas and that we did not exchange gifts. He asked me how I was feeling. I told him that I was hungry. I told him that my head, shoulders and neck hurt and that I was bleeding. In addition, I was fine and just wanted to lie down. Since I knew my husband, I asked him, "Who were those people?"

At first, John did not know what I was asking. However, I must have been pointing behind me because he answered that he did not know them. Then, he asked me what happened.

"I think I slipped on some ice and fell flat on my back. It knocked the wind out of me because I took in a huge breath before I opened my eyes. It's almost dark. What are we having for dinner? Did you make dinner?"

"Where is your insurance card?" he asked me.

"In my purse. Why?"

"Because I'm taking you to the hospital," he explained, pulling the car into the driveway. "Wait here!"

"Okay."

My husband left the Jeep running and got out. Running around the front of the car, he looked back and pointed. I could hear him tell me again to "wait here." All I could think was that I hoped he was taking me to dinner and that I could eat it without being sick. My head hurt.

As I waited in the car, my cell phone rang from my pocket. I answered the phone because it was my step-daughter, Brooke. "Hello?"

"Toni?" Brooke asked. "Where is Dad?"

"He's in the apartment," I explained. "Where are you?"

"I'm with Leah. I called and he didn't answer his phone."

"Did you call the apartment or his cell?"

"His cell," she said. "Where are you?"

"In the Jeep waiting for him," I explained.

"Where are you going?" she asked.

"Um…" I had not a clue where we were going. "I hope to dinner."

"What is wrong with you?" she asked.

"I hit my head," I said.

"Oh. Well, are you guys going to dinner?"

"Are you going to be home for dinner?" I countered.

"Well, that is why I was calling Dad," she explained, "I was hoping to stay at Leah's."

"Did you ask your Dad?" I asked.

"That's why I am calling you. I couldn't get a hold of Dad!"

"Oh, ok. Well, I will tell him when he comes back."

"Thanks."

She hung up and I forgot all about her call. John came back to the car and hopped in, handing me my purse. "So, where are we going to dinner?" I asked.

"We aren't going to dinner," he said with a laugh. "I am taking you to the hospital."

"Why?" I asked him.

"What day is it?" he asked me.

"Sunday?"

"Nope."

"Well, what day is it?" I asked.

"Thursday, January first."

"New Year's day?" I asked.

"Yes."

"Shit! Did I miss Christmas?"

"No, you did not miss Christmas." His voice was assuring, but amused. "I am taking you to the hospital to get checked out. Your head isn't working right now."

While I tried to absorb the fact that I forgot Christmas, I noticed that John was driving north towards town. He turned left on sixth. It is funny how the brain works, remembering one thing and forgetting another. As he drove west, I asked him, "Are you bringing me to Lakeview?"

"No. We're going to Holy Family."

"No!" I protested. "You can't take me there! They'll kill me there!"

It was sad and funny at the same time. I couldn't blame him for laughing. That was John. He found humor at the most inappropriate times. One time, he got the giggles in church during the readings because he thought of an episode of *"Seinfeld"* where Kramer was modeling underwear. He giggled for the rest of Mass. His laughing at me somehow kept me from panic. "They aren't going to kill you!"

"Can't you take me to Hudson?" I begged.

"I am not driving all the way to Hudson tonight. We're just going to get you checked out." He was pulling in the parking lot of the hospital in New Richmond. He parked in the lot, about two blocks away from the doors of the ER. Holding his arm, we made our way across the parking lot. I was so dizzy and my head was pounding.

"This better be quick! I'm starving," I told him as we reached the doors.

"Me too."

Chapter 2

It's Just Road Rash

When we got to the doors of the emergency entrance, John pressed the button for the intercom to the nurse's station. The years of high alert security were still upon us. My blue Disney 1968 Tigger™ jacket and camouflage sweatpants were not exactly threatening in a Wisconsin setting. Yet, I'm pretty sure my eyes reflected all the confusion and fear that I was feeling- to people who have been experiencing all sorts of crazy since September 11, 2001. They still buzzed us in the door and came to our aid.

Surprisingly, I felt the quiet of the ward immediately upon passing through the doors. It was like someone pressed the mute button on the remote control and shut all the sound off. Even the chatter in my head stopped, while John explained to the woman at the desk why we were there. I stood next to him, swaying slightly from the dizziness. "Do you need me to get a chair?" the nurse asked me.

"No," I answered, not knowing why they didn't have chairs there in the first place, "I can stand."

"Can you walk? I can get a wheelchair. We are going down the hall," she explained.

"I walked in here. I think I'm good."

They took me to a treatment room and had me sit on the bed. I pulled my jacket up over my head, almost falling to the floor from my seated position. John sat on a chair in the room, holding my purse and then, my jacket. He was shaking his head and laughing a little at me, as I tried to get my jacket off. The medical assistant had gone to get something to clean my head. "It's not funny, you jackass," I said. This only made him laugh outright.

The nurse, or medical assistant, (I am not sure what she was,) came back in to clean my head up. The sting of antiseptic burned along the base of my neck and up to the center of my cranium. I sat as still as I could, as she asked questions while she cleaned. "Do you hurt anywhere?"

"My neck and back. My left shoulder hurts," I told her. "My head feels like it is going to explode and I am nauseous."

The nurse finished with the antiseptic-wiping hell she was inflicting on me and asked me if I could tolerate some ice on my neck. When I told her I could, she left to get some, bringing it back in a short amount of time. "The doctor will see you when he is done with another patient. Just sit tight."

"Where the hell am I going to go?" I asked John after she left. "You have the keys and I know you aren't taking me out of here until someone looks at me." At his laughter, I asked, "What's so damn funny?"

"You, my little klutz."

"I'm hungry. Can we go yet?"

On his lap, John had a clipboard that was given to him by one of the staff. He was writing my information down, filling in the blanks. I closed my eyes and wanted to go to sleep. "Don't go to sleep," he told me. "We cannot go until after the doctor sees you. Besides, they have your insurance card."

I didn't remember giving them my card, "How the hell did they get that?"

"I gave it to Shannon."

"Who is Shannon?"

"The nurse that was just in here."

"We should have gone to Hudson. I'm afraid I'm not leaving here."

"Oh, for the love of God, you are leaving here with me."

"Now?"

"No."

"But, I'm hungry. We could go have a beer?" I asked hopefully. Johnny never turned down a beer!

"No."

"Hello there!" a guy with a cheesy mustache and balding head walked into the room. He had glasses, a tie and a stethoscope around his neck. He introduced himself as

Doctor Something-or-Other and I totally missed it. "I hear we had a bit of a fall?"

"Yes, I did."

"Can you tell me what happened?"

"Sure. I went for a walk," I explained. "I slipped on some ice and my feet flew out from under me. I fell flat on my back and head and got the wind knocked out of me. Now, I can't remember Christmas."

"Hmm..." the doctor was shining a light in my eyes.

"That makes me dizzy," I told him.

"I need to check your pupils."

"It makes me want to throw up on you."

"Oh," the doctor backed up a step, while Johnny laughed. "What's your name, Dear?"

I found it odd that this guy was calling me 'Dear' with my husband sitting there. He wasn't more than 10 years older than me, but he sounded like a grandpa. "Toni Geving."

"Do you know this guy here?"

"Yes. He's my husband."

"What's his name?"

"John Geving."

"Squeeze my hands," he instructed me. When I did, he said, "Good." He took out an instrument that looked like a circular fabric cutter with little spiky things on the wheel. He ran it up both arms and asked me if it felt different on either side. He pressed on both sides of my neck, my shoulder and back, all the while asking what hurt, didn't hurt, etc.

"What's your birthdate?"

"October 2?" I asked, more than answered.

"Are you sure about that?"

"I think so."

He asked me many questions to test my knowledge of current events. Who was the President of the United States? What was my address? Where did I fall? Then, he asked the question that I had been asking for over an hour, "What day is it?"

"January 1, 2009!" I said. John, who had been giggling in the chair, slapped his head and gave me a look that indicated he could not believe I got that right. How could I not?

"So, do you remember Christmas now?" the doctor asked.

"No."

"I think the memory loss is temporary and just short term."

"Really? But why do I not remember Christmas?"

"I don't know. But, you will."

"The only reason I remembered the date is because I asked before you came in here."

"I know," he smiled as he responded. "I heard you ask before I came in here."

"Can you tell me your name again?" I asked. He did give me his name again and I forgot it immediately.

With a bit of a shrug, he asked me a couple more questions. Some of them were repeats, but one of them was whether I had lost consciousness, or not. I remember telling him that I did not, but realized later that I probably did. If I just had the wind knocked out of me, the appearance of the woman and the guy blowing snow looming over me when I opened my eyes did not make sense. Maybe telling him I did not was what got me out of there in about an hour? At that point, I was not capable of concocting a lie to get us out of there quicker, but I would have if I could function in that capacity. I was hungry!

"Well, I think you have road rash and a concussion. We don't make anyone wake you up every hour anymore. You can take some Tylenol or ibuprofen for pain if you need it. I will release you to your husband. Shannon has some paperwork that she will bring back for you to sign and you can go home," he said.

When the nurse came back, she had a yellow sheet of paper with a list of concussion care instructions. One of the things listed on the sheet of paper was to watch for extreme tiredness, dizziness, and swelling. It also instructed the patient to not be alone and to have someone wake them every couple hours. "If the patient cannot be woken, seek immediate care or call 911, as brain hemorrhaging is possible." I was reading this sheet to John when we finally got home and getting a bit hysterical. "That quack told you not to wake me up! I am dizzy, sleepy and nauseous. My head feels like it is going to split open from the swelling along the base of my skull and he tells me to take ibuprofen?"

"Calm down," John told me. "Go to bed and sleep. I will wake you up before bed."

"I told you to take me to Hudson. If you need to call an ambulance in the middle of the night, you make sure they don't take me to Holy Family!"

"Yes, Dear."

"I'm hungry, dammit!"

"So am I."

"I am not fixing dinner. You can do it!"

"Go lay down and I will make us some soup and sandwiches," John said. "I have to call Brooke and find out where she is."

"Yeah, I wondered where she was," I said, as I grabbed an ice pack from the freezer to wrap around my neck and head. "I am going to sit down while you make soup."

Grilled cheese sandwiches with tomato soup are one of my favorite comfort foods. While the cat purred on the couch next to me, I dunked grilled cheese in my soup. It was about 9:30 by this time and football was still playing on the television. We were sitting in the living room on our side-by-side chairs that were like recliners. The entrance to our apartment came into the living room from the sidewalk outside. As we sat there eating, the front door opened and a petite blonde girl walked through the door with a string of keys. She was wearing a plaid, hooded coat and tennis shoes. "Who are you?" I asked, as she walked into the place like she lived there.

"What do you mean?" she asked.

My husband was looking at me like I had two heads. Maybe he was suffering from answering all my questions? "Do you know who that is?" he asked.

"What do you mean?" Blondie said again.

"No?" I said in the form of a question, wondering if I should know her. I looked at her a minute and knew that I'd seen the face before, but could not put the name to it. "Who are you?"

"That's Brooke?" he said, as a way of asking if that made sense.

"Oh my God!" Brooke said, "What is going on?"

John held up a finger, waiting for me to recognize this girl. When I didn't say anything, he turned to Brooke and asked her, "Where have you been? I thought you were going

20

to be home by seven. When I called your phone, it went straight to voice mail."

"I called and talked to Toni!"

"Oh yeah!" I finally realized who she was, "Brooke!"

"When did you call?" John asked, pinching the bridge of his nose with his thumb and forefinger.

"At about four," she said. "She said you were going to dinner and you went inside to get her purse."

Both of them were looking at me suspiciously. "I don't remember that!"

"I asked you where you were," Brooke continued, "and you said you were in the Jeep waiting for Dad to take you to dinner."

"Well, he didn't take me to dinner. He took me to New Richmond hospital and almost got me killed!"

"What do you mean?" Brooke said again.

John proceeded to explain the events of the last few hours to his daughter. I could tell he was trying to make light of it, though he was concerned. Or, he was tired of answering the same questions repeatedly. First, me asking if I had missed Christmas and then his daughter asking, "What do you mean?" In fact, I think I was talking non-stop before Brooke came in and he was probably just tired of the whole thing. When he finished the story, Brooke went to her room.

"Dear, you need to go to bed. You look like hell and I will have to wake you in a couple hours."

"Why?" I asked.

"Because the directions say so."

Agreeing to go to bed was the easiest thing to do. I was exhausted, my head hurt and the soup was not sitting nicely in my stomach. I bent over to kiss him good-night and just about landed in his lap. "Whoa there!" he laughed. "Do you need some help to bed?" It was sad, but I did. It was even worse that he was laughing while he was being nice. I was so confused!   But, he was the one person that I knew would be there. I trusted him.

Of course, I did not remember talking earlier to her on the phone and I did not tell John that she had called. I remember having a couple discussions with John and her about this later. I don't remember when I actually recalled the memory of her phone call. Yet, we joked about it for a week when I did.

Due to our inability to have children, we created an imaginary brother for Brooke, named Brach. Whenever Brooke would do something that was less than what we expected of her, we would tease her that Brach didn't do this type of thing. So, when I remembered that Brooke had called me, I jokingly said, "Brach would have called back and talked to your dad!" Now, this only made me wonder how I remembered an imaginary, younger brother for Brooke, but not that Christmas actually happened 6 days before? Why did my brain recall random made-up things, but not produce the answer to a simple math equation like two plus two equals four?

Chapter 3

Stop Whispering!

The second day of January that year was a Friday and most people who had jobs were required to go back to work. The company where I worked was no exception. In 2009, I had taken the day off. My husband, on the other hand, was going to work. After waking me up several times the night before, he was up at 5:30 A.M. to shower and go to work. Before he left, he woke me up, kissed me and told me he loved me. "I will call you at lunch."

The day was filled with funky dreams. I don't know that I ever heard the phone ring, let alone got up to answer it. I don't know where Brooke was all day. When John got home at 4:00, he came in frantic and woke me up. "Hey, are you okay!" he said, shaking me to make sure I was awake.

"What?" I asked him. Why did he look like a crazy man? Why was he shaking me? Did he want me to throw up? "John, I'm awake! Stop shaking me, or I am going to throw up!"

He sighed and watched as I sat up in bed and closed my eyes. I was waiting for the room to stop spinning around. I was waiting for the voices to stop chattering. What the heck was going on? My head felt like it was going to split in half and spill my brains all over the bed. When I felt it was safe, I opened my eyes to look at him.

"Have you been sleeping all day?"

"I don't know. What time is it?" I said quietly.

"It is four o'clock."

"Then, yes. I have been sleeping all day." I did not realize how odd that was for me.

"Do you remember talking to me earlier?"

"When you called me on your lunch?"

"Yes."

"I remember."

"You told me that you were going to try eating something."

"I did?" I asked.

"Yes. What did you eat?"

"I had some toast, I think."

"You don't look so good," he said. "Do you think you can handle a shower?"

"Gee thanks, John!" I said. "So, I don't look good and I need a shower?"

He laughed and assured me that was not what he meant. Apparently, he felt I might feel a bit better if I showered and got up for a little bit. "I will make something for you to eat while you are in the shower."

"Okay."

When I got out of the shower, John told me that Brooke was at her friend's house for the weekend and that he was going to work. I must have given him a confused look because he said, "The bar?"

"You are going to the bar?"

"I'm going to cook at the Sports Club. I do that every Friday night."

"Oh." For no reason, I started to cry. I didn't want him to go. I didn't want him to leave me there alone. My whole body ached. The back of my head still stung from the shower. When I moved, I got dizzy. I couldn't tell him not to go to work, could I?

"What's the matter?" he asked, wrapping his arms around me and hugging me close to his chest. He was taller than me and could put his chin on top of my head. When he did that, I felt a sharp pain go down through my skull and into the back of my neck. But, it felt so good to have him holding me that I didn't want to tell him it hurt.

"I don't want you to leave me alone," I cried.

As was his habit, he tried to joke that I would probably sleep the whole time he was gone. When that didn't stop the tears, he said, "I'll be back later. You can watch whatever you want on TV."

"I feel so dumb. I don't even know why I am crying."

"It's your nugget. You are still confused."

"There is so much noise in here," I said, "I don't know if I can concentrate on the TV."

Half laughing again, he asked, "what do you mean there is so much noise in here? It's quiet."

Again, I was confused by this. "The phone rings, the dishwasher, the washing machine, the television and the whispering. Can't you hear that? The phone drives me nuts!"

"What whispering?" he asked.

"And all the lights floating around- what do you mean, what whispering? Can't you hear it?" I asked.

"No. And, the lights," he said, "are you talking about the colors you see?"

"No..." though, the lights I was seeing were sometimes colored, they were extremely bright and hard to look at and they seemed to be walking through the apartment, as if they were human. All of them talked to me in a low whisper, though I could not quite understand what they were saying. That made listening to the other sounds more difficult. I tried to explain this to him, but he did not understand the jumble of words that were coming out of my mouth.

"Was that even English?" he asked.

"I'm sorry. I can't seem to make sense of this."

"Maybe, after you eat, you should just go back to bed?" He had to leave, as he was already late. "I can call Dana and see if he needs me."

"Never mind, just go to work," I said in a pouty voice.

He kissed me on the lips, telling me that he would be home right after he was done working and that he loved me. "Hamburger Helper™ is on the stove and I turned it off." He was off to work again, leaving me alone to watch the television and eat Hamburger Helper™.

Helping myself to a plate of Hamburger Helper and a glass of milk, I sat down on the couch and turned on the television. The volume was so loud I had to immediately press the down button until the sound of the television was just over the whispers. Then, I had to find a non-sports related channel. I had no ambition to watch football, basketball, or any other ball. I watched some early evening reruns on ABC Family while eating my dinner.

The weekend went a bit like Friday did. I slept a lot, forgot things, and really could not make any sudden movements. At one point, John drove me to Stillwater. I think we were going to have breakfast, but I don't remember for sure why we were there. John turned onto the main street that went through downtown Stillwater. We had to stop at a light. I looked to my right and saw a store front with pots and pans of many colors in the window called "The Chef's Gallery."

The city of Stillwater, Minnesota was a mix of old world setting and new-fangled Yuppy. There were old buildings along the St. Croix River with walkways, antique shops, good food stops and a lift bridge that went up for the boats in the summer. That morning, I looked over at the little shop on the corner, with windows on two sides and a narrow alley running next to the building up a steep inclining hill. I knew this place. It was like a puzzle piece clicked into the space in my memory that knew this place.

The sensations of walking into that store flooded through my head as the memory came quickly to every sense. First, the smell of spices came to my nose, mingling together so that I could not discern which was more intoxicating. Then, bright colors beckoned me to touch and weigh something in my hand. The cute gadgets and unique tools called me to buy. These senses came to my memory in an instant of seeing the corner. "I know that place!" I said excited. "John! I know that place!"

From the driver's seat, John sighed as he nodded. "Yes, you do."

The happiness I felt from seeing something that was familiar lasted about a block. As I remembered that memory, I remembered another. "I sent someone there when they were visiting?" I asked him, knowing I was right.

"Yes," he confirmed. He watched me jump on the seat a bit before he said, "Mike and Diana. Stacey's Mom and Dad."

"Was that at our wedding?" I asked.

"Yes."

"Oh my God, Mike's dead!" At that moment, I was hit with the most profound feeling of sadness. I cannot even explain how it feels to remember things backwards and not really remember anything at all. I felt the pain of losing someone important, yet could not quite remember him. I knew he liked to cook and did it well. I remembered him making me a cheese cake and that I ate that cheese cake with a nurse in the hospital. I remembered laughter and a little red car. I remembered he was important somehow. John watched me as tears came down my face. "Why am I crying?" I asked him. "Why does it feel like he just died?"

The hand that reached out and touched me on my leg was warm and kind. "It's alright," he patted my leg. "You are just remembering things."

"I know Stacey is important to me. I just can't remember why. I can't picture her face."

After explaining to me that Stacey was my best friend from college and had been the maid of honor in our wedding, I did not feel any better. I could not understand why my head would not remember these people that were a part of my life.

Though, I was assured by my husband I would remember soon, I still could not understand why some things were there and others were not.

The next day was Monday. Although I was still dizzy and had a headache, I told John I was going to work because I had no vacation time and we needed the money. So, he made sure I was up and getting ready. Due to his need to keep an eye on me, his sleeping had been disrupted and he was somewhat surly in the morning. We both were getting dressed when I looked at him and asked, "What do I do?"

He was in the process of putting his shirt on when I asked the question. He stopped moving with his arms in the sleeves. "What do you mean?"

"What do I do at my job?"

"You talk on the phone all day to people."

"Why the hell would I do that?!" I asked, disgusted. "I hate talking on the phone!"

"Ah," John was looking at me with a mix of incredulousness and concern that would have been comical if I was in my right mind, "do you even know where you are going?"

"Yes. I'm going to Woodbury."

Shaking his head, he grabbed me by the arms and looked into my eyes. "Are you sure you are okay to drive?"

I gave him a kiss on the lips and assured him that I was fine, even though I had no clue why I would work at a job where I talk on the phone all day. Then, he asked me, "Are you working tonight?"

"Massage?" I asked.

"You remember that?"

"Yes."

"How does that work?" John wondered aloud. We had been noticing that my brain had gaps of memory that seemed to be erased. My brain replayed some memories clearly, while others seemed to be wiped out by a magic eraser. For the most part, he was good-natured about it. However, the memory was not the only thing impacted by the blow to my head, which we were slowly finding out. My personality had changed, too.

With an "I love you," a hug and a kiss, we headed out the door. He had started the vehicles, so that they would warm up. His daughter had already left the house, after complaining that she did not want to go to school. I got in the car and headed out to work. It was still dark and I just drove.

When I got into the Jeep, the radio was belting out some country tune. Immediately, I switched it off, as I could not concentrate with all the noise. The voices were still whispering at a distance and I could not deal with them and the radio. The lights floating around in the car were almost as distracting. So, I kept my eyes on the road, looking for deer and things that might cause me more issues. I followed the cars through the backwoods, over the Willow River, past the State park and out to 94.   At some point, I realized I needed to stop and pump gas. I knew exactly where to go, getting off the interstate in Woodbury and pulling into a Super America gas station.

After pumping gas, I went into the gas station, got a cup of coffee and paid for my gas. Heading back out to the car, I realized how tired I was when I buckled my seatbelt. Then, wondered, "Was I going to work, or home from work?" I guessed I was going to work and turned right to go west again. My head was pounding again and I was dizzy. A new wave of nausea came with the dizziness.

Pulling into my usual parking space, I got out of the car and ran my key card to unlock the door. I knew how to get into the building. I knew where I sat. I walked around the corner and sat down next to a dark-haired woman I had been working next to for 3 years. I had no idea who she was. I recognized the gentle eyes and knew I could trust her, but did not know her name. I turned to my computer screen and phone and had no clue what I was supposed to do with either of them. "Happy New Year, Toni!" the woman said to me. "Did you have a good weekend?"

I turned to the woman with tears starting and did not know what to say to her. I just looked at her and tried to piece a coherent sentence together.

"What's wrong?" she asked.

"I don't know who you are." I started to cry.

"What?" she asked. "It's Barb."

"Well, Barb," I said through my growing panic, "I fell and hit my head on Thursday. I don't know what I'm supposed to do here."

"You need to talk to Colleen."

"But, I don't have vacation," I said.

Somehow, she directed me to Colleen, who was on her way to ask me to get on the phone when I met her in the hallway. I didn't know what to tell her, so I just spilled out my story. Then, I explained that I did not know how to get on the phone. I waited at my desk while she went to "check on something," telling me she would come back.

Barb was taking phone calls, while I sat there and tried to figure out what I was supposed to do. I listened to her half-heartedly, as she explained the foreign language of long term care insurance to some elderly caller on the phone. I had no clue what she was talking about. Did I even know any of this?

The noise was starting to get to me. The phones rang around me and on my desk. The lights flitted around me as I felt the panic crawling up my spine. I was going to completely lose it any minute. At one point, I sent my new- found, old buddy, Barb, a silent plea for help. I was about ready to blow, until she turned to me and said, "It is okay, Toni."

All of a sudden, people were coming over to me and asking questions, which I could not answer. Barb was deflecting as much as she could when she wasn't on the phone. But, I was really feeling overwhelmed by all of these strangers who seemed to know me, though I did not know them. The fact that they expected me to answer these questions really bothered me. How was I supposed to answer them?

Finally, Colleen came back to my desk and told me that I had some time available that I could use. She said that I should get into the doctor and get checked and call when I got home. Hadn't I told her already that I had been to the doctor? I packed up my bag.

"Are you sure you can drive?" asked Barb.

"I got here, didn't I?" I asked. Though, I didn't really arrive there in one piece. There were parts of me missing. My brain was not all there. So, I drove home, after promising I would make an appointment with my doctor and call my boss to tell her I had made it home. I got home and went to bed- forgetting my promise to call my boss and make an appointment with my doctor.

Chapter 4

Work Is Necessary

When John got home that Monday night to find me sleeping, he realized that something was seriously wrong. He woke me up and asked me why I was home. I explained to him what happened. With a shake of his head, he asked if I had called the doctor. When I told him I did not remember, he got on the phone. I had an appointment for Wednesday by the time he was done.

On Wednesday, I went into work and explained that I was going to the doctor that morning. The human resource department was involved by then, telling me that I needed a doctor's note to come back to work. I had no vacation, no sick leave available, so I was not getting paid for any of my absence. This was not a good thing for our budget. We had survived on less, but we were trying to keep ahead of the debt collector. This seems like a never-ending story for many people.

During the first part of the week, I realized that I had my own massage business in town. I remembered that I massaged after my full-time job most evenings of the week and Saturdays. In fact, I remembered everything about massage. However, I went to my full-time job with a company

I had worked with for 5 years and I couldn't remember how to log into my computer. I could not remember how to log onto my phone, or what I did. Every time I asked someone at my full-time job what I did, I got a different answer. Supposedly, I was a "Subject Matter Expert". Yet, I had no clue what subject matter I was an expert on, or what relevance it had to the company.

When I went into the doctor's office that morning, I still had a headache and vertigo. Some of my past had pieced itself together, but there were huge voids. It was so odd that many individuals thought I was faking the memory loss. So, as I told my general practitioner about the last week of events, she shook her head and kind of laughed. "It's like a bad soap opera," she laughed.

"I know!" I agreed. "How do I remember some people and not others? How do I remember where I work, but not what I do? And, why do I only remember certain people?"

After having my head poked, a light shined in my eyes, reflexes checked and all the other questions answered, I was sent to get an immediate MRI to check for brain bleeds. Or, maybe just to check for my brain? I'm not entirely sure which was the goal, but I'm sure both were important. I asked her for a note to go back to work. She said that she would give me that, but I needed to find a ride going forward, as I should not be driving with vertigo and the headache. Plus, she would not allow me to go back until the following week.

One of the things I talked to the doctor about was my sensitivity to sound. What I did not tell her was that I continually heard whispering that seemed to be directed at me. I could not listen to the radio. I could not stand phone noises. I had a hard time with anything on my head. In addition, I did tell her about the "spots" of light that I saw floating around. I did not tell her that on occasion, they looked and felt like people. At the time, I was afraid that my accident had brought on some type of crazy that I didn't want diagnosed by the medical profession. All I could think about was being put into some type of mental institution because I was "hearing voices" and "seeing things".

When I got done with everything, I stopped at the office, informing them that I could not come back to work until the following Monday. I explained that I would have to find a ride and didn't know how I was going to do that. I was given some names of people that I could try by my boss. One of them was supposedly related to me. John confirmed that. I was so thankful that I had him and knew who he was! He seemed to take my mental departure in stride and helped me as much as he could. Yet, there were days when I think he wondered where his wife went. He just loved me and told me everything would be fine in a few weeks.

At some point, John encouraged me to contact his aunt and see if I could get a ride with her to work. His Aunt Nancy was part of a car pool and she said she would check to see if I could hitch a ride. I agreed to pay $5 for each day I rode with them. The first day, I was out at the curb when the truck pulled up. I got into the back seat with all these people that I did not know. I recognized the face of a couple people, but the names were sketchy. On the way to work that morning, I explained why I needed the ride. The dizziness, the memory loss, and the confusion about what I do for our mutual employer came out in the 45 minutes ride. I got there a little early and was able to keep the voices at bay.

The most frustrating thing about memory loss for me was the fact that I knew the faces of the people I talked to, but the names would not connect. Or, knowing that there was a chain of events that happened and I could remember only parts of it. As I was getting coffee for myself in the company break room, a woman came up to me and said, "Jamie told me about your memory loss. That must be really tough?"

"Yeah," I said. "It is really hard when you recognize the face, but cannot associate a name."

"That sucks!" she said, as she walked out of the break room without telling me her name.

As I stood there, looking at the door close behind her, I couldn't help but think my day was going to go much like I expected. It was going to really be taxing on my already spinning brain. Will I recognize anyone? I will say that I remembered Barb from the two days I was in the office briefly. She was so helpful and understanding of my condition. She tried to assist me in remembering my log on passwords for the computer and phone. When people came to me with questions, she would see my confused and panicked look and help direct them where they needed to go. Or, she would just say, "That information is available in the online library," and shoo them away from me. I was blessed by that woman, in more ways than I can remember.

It took me two weeks to remember where my password for my computer was hidden. It took me months to be okay with the phones ringing and the white noise. I was able to take phone calls after about 4 weeks. But, every time I asked someone what I did for the company, I would get a different answer. When I could log into my computer, my boss told me to go read the manuals online and "get back up to speed" on what I do. Yet, I had to go to one of the trainers to find out where the manuals could be found online. There was no sympathy to the fact that I could not remember what it was I was a Subject Matter Expert on. It seemed counter-productive for me to learn everything all over, by myself.

Quite frankly, it was the first thing that proved to me that they would replace me in a heartbeat if they could.

Every day I went to work, I asked my husband, "Do I have to go?"

Of course, he told me that I had to go. Then, he would try to reassure me that I would remember something. "You will start to remember stuff. You remember massage."

"Yes," I said. "But, I like massage!"

One night, about three weeks after the accident, I came home from working in my studio at the chiropractic office. John was sitting on the couch eating something he had prepared for dinner. As I sat down in the chair next to him, he said, "Do you remember that every night, after you get home from working at the clinic, you give me a massage?"

I looked at his sincere face and immediately realized he was joking. "You are full of shit!" I said. Then, I started laughing with him. It was the perfect thing for him to say to me at that moment. I was feeling so taxed and run down. "Did you think I would actually believe that?"

"It was worth a shot! My shoulder is killing me!" he said, between snorts of laughter.

I immediately had a red flag come up. "What do you mean; your shoulder is killing you?" I asked him.

"It is."

"How long has it been killing you?"

"For a couple weeks," he explained. "I told you about it before Christmas."

"You need to come in, so I can work on it."

"I have a headache too."

"Are you going to get that checked?"

"Quit being such a worrywart," he said. "I will be fine."

I rattled off several things that shoulder pain could indicate. It was his left shoulder, neck and head. I kept hearing "blood flow" from the whispering. I kept thinking that referred pain was from an issue with his heart. Shoulder pain and a headache can be indicative of a stroke, too. "John, you need to have that checked!"

This argument went on for a few days. I was always "nagging" him to get his health issues checked. He was always telling me to stop worrying. I did get him into the office and gave him a few massages. I had found that I couldn't raise my arms above my head without causing the vertigo to come back. The chiropractor I worked with actually was doing some positioning movements that helped me. John was my rock. He was the one I called when I was freaking out. He was the one to calm me down. He brought humor and levity to the situation every day. There were days when I did not think I would have a job anymore. I wasn't too upset about it, as I didn't know what I really did for the company.

At some point in January, I took a client at the massage school that I attended in Hudson. I rented a room one night after work and my client met me there. After the massage, I went to Fleet Farm to get some cat food for the monster of a cat that lived with us. On my way home, in the dark, I somehow got lost. I could not remember the way home from Hudson. I took a wrong turn somewhere and ended up in some back country neighborhood with 3 acre lots. Nothing looked familiar! What was I going to do? Of course, I called John.

"Hello?" he sighed, like he was wondering what mess he had to deal with now. I could tell he was tired.

"I'm lost," I said, trying not to let him hear the panic in my voice.

"What do you mean, you are lost?" he asked, laughing.

"Dammit! Don't laugh at me! I'm fucking lost!" I cried. So much for not letting him hear the panic in my voice!

There was a pause on the other end and a sigh. "Well, where are you?"

"I don't know. I'm lost."

"I don't know how I am going to help you, if you cannot give me basic information."

I didn't know if I was going to cry or hang up and just not go home. How could I explain to him how scared and panicked I was without verbally ripping his head off at that moment? It would be so easy for me to just stop the vehicle by the side of this residential road and sit there until it was light out. Anger and frustration were not something that I was capable of dealing with together at that moment. I opened my mouth and could not stop the words from coming out, "Don't be an ass! I am afraid."

"Well, Dear, where did you go after you left Fleet Farm?" His manner was calm and maybe a little resigned when he asked the questions, but I could tell he was trying not to make me even more hysterical. "Did you turn right or left when you left the parking lot?"

"Left."

"OK, so did you make a right when you got to the stop light?"

"Yes."

"Tell me from there where you went."

"I went past a hospital," I told him.

"Good. Did you go through a stop sign?"

"I stopped and turned right."

"By the movie theater?"

"Yes."

"Can you get back to that stop sign?"

"I think so. I have to remember how I got where I am."

"Turn around and go back the way you came," he instructed.

In January, it is very dark in Wisconsin. Most of the western cities are small, so the light pollution is minimal. The nice thing is that the stars on a clear night are incredible. Without a moon, it is like looking at a jewel-encrusted black carpet. Many times, I have seen one of those jewels shoot across the sky in a falling arch. This night was overcast and dark. I did not recognize anything in the dark. When I weaved my way back to the stop sign, I was happy I could tell him where I was.

"Turn right," he instructed.

I turned right and drove. I explained to him that I was coming to another stop sign and he told me to turn left after I'd turned right again. "Turn around and go straight." I described what I was seeing and he kept asking me if I knew where I was. Of course, I didn't. So, he stayed on the phone with me for 15 miles, until I found my way home. How could I not love this man? I had just called him an ass and totally melted down on him, and he remained calm and showed me he loved me by guiding me home. When I walked in the door, he encircled me in his arms and let me cry. I didn't know why I needed that from him until later. He was my safety net, when I felt like I had nothing safe.

"What do you think the problem was tonight?" he asked me after holding me for a few minutes. I could hear the amusement in his voice.

"Nothing looked familiar in the dark," I said.

"You do know you drive that way to work every day, right?"

"Now, I do."

"Stop your blubbering," he said, wiping my tears with his finger. "You are going to remember everything!"

"I hope so!" I said.

At the time, I just did not see that I would remember everything. Even now, I believe that the unimportant stuff will not ever come back, as my soul released it. It wasn't serving my highest purpose. So, why should I remember that?

Chapter 5

I Can Do That

Two nights later, my friend, Tara, had asked me to come to her home and help her clear some low- level energy that was taking up space in her home. I asked my step-daughter, Brooke, to come with me. The request was more because I was afraid of not finding my way to Menomonie and home again. It was Friday night and there was no way that John could talk me home from there. However, Brooke could help me get home. So, off we went.

There was not ever a question that I could successfully help with this task. I don't remember how I knew what I was doing, or why it seemed like I'd been doing this for many years. I just knew that this was like breathing for me. The voices in my head assured me that they knew what to do and they would be helping me. Although I was still sensitive to the sound and the lights that I seemed to hear and see all the time, I still did not understand them, or know who, or what they were. Plus, I sure as hell was not going to tell anyone, especially my doctor, that I was hearing voices and seeing things! My husband already knew and just seemed to take it in stride.

When I told John I was going to go clear a house, his only question to me was, "Are you sure you are up for that?"

"Yeah, I think so," I said.

"That doesn't sound too convincing," he laughed. Then, he kissed me and headed off to work in Hudson, telling me to be careful. "I know you are going to be late because you will be with Tara. Watch for deer on your drive home!"

Menomonie was a forty-five minute drive east of New Richmond. The main interstate that goes east through Wisconsin cuts through some beautiful rolling hills that were created by the Wisconsin glacier. The hills were melt-off spots where the glacier dropped rich sediment that made this area fabulous for farming. Every season presented impressive scenery along the drive from rich, vibrant colors of Autumn, lush green in Summer, wildflowers in Spring and pristine white and blue in Winter. On this night, it was clear and the moon reflected off the snow-covered fields.

Brooke and I found our way with the directions that Tara had given me. We pulled into her driveway and parked next to a big, twisted box elder tree. The tree was twisted like a tornado up the trunk and had an eerie look and feel to it. In my ear, I distinctly heard "vortex". As I was wondering what that meant, an answer came to me that it was a point of energy transfer that could be useful in bringing lower-level energy to and from the home.

A healer herself, Tara had already started using essential oils to clear some of the energy. Frankincense was warming in a burner. She had sea salt and sage bundles, water and candles. I came armed with alcohol and Epsom salt. Though, I did not know how I knew to bring these items. I also had an angel book and knew I needed to call on a few key players here. I didn't know how to explain to anyone how I knew which spirits to call in, or that I could see them there. I felt them and saw so many other people in her house and around me all the time.

The Archangels are the most glorious beings I've ever seen. I had a special affinity to Michael. While I was in massage school, I was not seeing spirit the same way I see spirit now. When Michael presented himself to me, I felt a shift in the energy of the room. Yet, the one thing that I did see when he came into presence with me was his sword. The long, powerful instrument was green in color for me. Yet, these generals of God all have their own personalities and specialties.

As I mentioned, I had no idea how I knew how to call for their help, but I do recall Tara knowing who would help. Michael's general color was indigo- that color between a navy blue and purple. However, he also had a red cloak that fastened at the top of his neck with a tie string. I do not know exactly where under that cloak he kept it, but he carried a shield as impressive as his sword. I asked for his protection while I went through the house to see what was there.

After this particular clearing, I was told by a colleague that I could go directly to God to clear the energy. Most Christians who have studied the Bible believe that no demon can stay when God is invoked. At the time, I believed the same thing. Since then, I have not found that to be completely true. All I knew was that this work was powerful and seemed to come naturally to me. My Catholic upbringing did not adequately prepare me for this.

The first thing I noticed inside the house was an energetic stickiness that just was not healthy. It had the same quality of the month-old bag of baby carrots in the refrigerator. It looked wet at first glance, but was slimy to the feel. This sticky mass of goo was not throughout the whole house, but was concentrated in the downstairs level. There was other energy there, too. Some of the lower-level, darker stuff, felt foreign and unfamiliar to me. This energy was not from my light-hearted friend and her children. They could feel it. This was the reason they called for help.

My daughter, Brooke, walked through the house with me. When I asked her if she noticed anything, she stated that her nose was tingling and that she felt something "icky." She was right. It was definitely icky. Tara could feel the heaviness and her children could see shadows and odd things in various places of the house. Some of the energy was identified as her son, who had passed. Other energy was from her spouse, who had served several tours in the Middle East with the Army. Regardless of where this all came from, it seemed to move through the rooms of the house. It needed to be cleared.

I can tell you that I did not know what to expect that night. I was completely confident in my abilities to clear the space, as long as the resident occupants were not inviting it back. Yet, I had no clue why I could feel this confidence, as I could not recall how I came to know how to do what I was doing. I knew that I used the elements of air, fire, water, mineral and metal. There were areas of the house where the smoke from the fire highlighted faces. At one point, there was even a noose in a closet. I just kept moving the energy towards the door and the twisted tree.

When we finished, the space felt better. There was some residual stickiness, but by that time I was feeling the effects of my work and I still had a 45- mile drive home. We left quite late, and I remember going to bed when I got home. I believe sleep came quickly that night. There were many times when it did not come that quickly.

On the last Sunday of the month, my family collected themselves at my mother's house for Potluck Sunday. Every month, we assembled for a meal and birthday cake for all of the birthdays in the month. Two days after clearing the house, John, Brooke and I travelled to Bloomington, Minnesota to the home where I grew up for Potluck Sunday. As it was January, we were celebrating my younger sister's birthday and my mother's. This was the first time seeing my family in person since my head injury.

I had no problem recognizing my mother and siblings. However, I became very confused and upset with myself when I could not remember the names of my sister's children. My oldest brother, Bruce, found me crying in the hallway and asked me what was wrong. I explained to him that I did not know their names. "It's no big deal. Their names are Abby, Gareth and Zoë. There is no reason to cry," he told me in a tone that made me feel as if he was scolding me.

During this learning period, it was hard for me to explain that these little memory lapses were frustrating. Most people could not understand why I would remember one thing and forget something seemingly obvious, like the names of my nieces and nephew. How do I explain to my husband that I cannot do math in my head anymore? Why had my personality changed? And, why the hell do I not remember Christmas? Despite all the assurances that my memory would come back, I was afraid that it would not. When it came back, would I find out that I didn't really know any of these people?

It was John who came to me and told me, "I think I will take over the bills for a while."

"Why?" I asked, as I handed him the checkbook.

"We are having some errors in our checking account and I want you to keep giving me receipts."

"Is this because I cannot add and subtract in my head anymore?" I asked.

A smart-ass by nature, my husband asked, "Could you ever add and subtract in your head?" I hit him in the arm as he laughed at himself. Even as I did, I knew that balancing the checkbook was something I would never want to do again. I easily handed over that duty to John.

Sometime in the end of January, I had re-learned my job well enough to be able to take questions from the co-workers. For the most part, I was knowledgeable and felt better about fielding questions. Piece by piece, it made sense that I was in the position I was because of the stuff I knew. It was still there, but I could not remember how to access it and review it in my head.

All my superiors wanted me to pick up a phone and decrease the queue. At one point, I was actually told to "fake it until I make it." Clearly, that was how everyone stayed in that company. In that time I was teaching myself my job, I found that most of the people I worked with had no clue about what I did there. I wondered how that was possible. I wondered if any one of them could (or would) come into that building, feeling totally lost and vulnerable, and read material that felt and sounded foreign in order to keep their job. I felt like I would be fired because I was not faking it well enough. Nobody ever felt the need to correct that thinking. My boss even told me that if I was not able to do my job, they would have to find someone else, as they did not have anyone who could train me.

Why was that? Evidently, I was the only one that had the knowledge that my position required and not one of the superiors could train me. So, if I was unable to recall the info or train myself, I would have been fired.

On February 2, the company I worked for terminated 25 people in the company and announced changes. I sat in my corner desk, by the window and realized that I had somehow dodged a bullet. An hour after that announcement was made via e-mail, my husband called me on my office phone to tell me that he had just gotten laid off. The economy was about to take another downturn toward depression and we were in it. I cried for a minute and John said, "We'll be fine. I've already called to adjust the payments on my student loans. Plus, I have my resume out."

"Plus, if I die, you have my life insurance," I said to him.

"What?" he asked. I could tell he was not following me.

"I have life insurance, so you would be ok."

"Toni, what are you talking about?" he asked. "You are kind of scaring me."

"I don't know," I said into the phone. It was the truth, too. I had no clue why the thought came in through the top of my head and out the mouth. This coming into my head at all really confused me.

"I have to get back to work, John," I said. "Can we talk about this when I get home?"

"All right, drive home carefully."

"I will."

The same thought kept resurfacing in my consciousness. All the way through my day, I wondered why I was obsessed with counting the ways to save my husband from dealing with all of this. I could have had a brain bleed and died from my head injury, but I didn't. I could have succumbed to breast cancer ten years earlier, too. But, I didn't. How many times do we stare death in the face and get to say, "Sorry, I am not ready to go yet." And, more importantly, where did the thought that we do have a choice to leave come from anyway? Why did I know that we do have the choice to stay or go?

As I drove home, I asked myself, "Are you suicidal?" It was such a sickening thought, that I knew that I wasn't. Yet, it got me thinking about how these thoughts even came into my head. Why would I even think these things? Were these actually my thoughts? I did not know. There were many things that were happening that I could not explain. It was so loud in my head all the time and I saw so much going on around me, I really hated even thinking about all of this.

When I got home, John was waiting for me. He was sitting on the couch with his legs crossed; flipping channels on the television in his camouflage sweatpants. I came in and said hello. He got up, following me into the bedroom.

"I need to talk to you, Toni," he said, in a voice that was way too serious for my husband.

I turned to look at him, while stripping out of my work clothes. He grabbed me by the shoulders and hugged me close, pinning my arms to my sides. "What are you doing?"

"I don't want you avoiding me."

"I am not avoiding you. I have to pee and would like to get changed so I can do that," I explained, annoyed that he still held my arms down at my sides.

He kissed the tip of my nose and let go of me. He watched me change and sat down on the bed. I went into the bathroom and came out to find him in the same spot. He patted the bed next to him, inviting me to sit down.

As I sat down, I looked at his face. He was way too serious. "What is going on?"

"I need you to explain yourself."

"Huh?" I asked.

"The comment you made earlier about life insurance policies."

"I don't know that I can explain that comment. It just came out the mouth before I even thought about it."

He turned to me and said, "I realize that we don't have it easy, but I don't ever want to do this without you. I want you to know that we are going to be all right."

I sighed and tried to look anywhere but into his eyes. I had no clue if he would understand anything I said because I was so unsure of what to say. The last thing I wanted to do was alienate my husband. Yet, I had to explain to him what I was experiencing and try to make him understand that I was not considering offing myself. How do I explain to him all the strange things that are going on in my head?

"Tell me what is going on!"

"What do you mean?" I asked.

"Since your head injury, I know you have been confused and scared. Your personality has changed. You don't talk to me the same. Plus, I feel like you are hiding something, or are not telling me something?"

I could not avoid telling him anything anymore. No matter how completely crazy I sounded, I had to explain to him what was happening. I was afraid to confide in him about the voices in my head and the lights I was seeing. Would he commit me to a mental institution? No, he was my husband. Besides, he needed my income to balance our budget. We both couldn't be out of work! "I don't know where to start," I admitted.

"How about we start with the comment you made about the life insurance?"

"I don't know where that came from," I said. I hoped my look was imploring him to believe me. "It just came out of my mouth. I thought of it all the way home and don't know why I said it. I am glad I am here."

He sighed and wiped tears away from my cheeks. I did not even realize that I was crying. His silence encouraged me to continue. Though he did not say anything aloud, I heard his voice in my head say, "Please just keep talking."

"So, you know I can't listen to the radio when I drive anymore?" I asked. At his nod, I continued, "well, it is more than that. I can't stand being on the phone. The talking in my ears is constant. I'm hearing voices, John. And that is only half the problem."

"You've yelled at Brooke a couple times because of her ring tone."

"It's fucking obnoxious! But, yes, all sounds drive me nuts. I can't concentrate. Then, there are the lights floating around everywhere."

"What?" he asked. "Maybe you had a retina detach from the blow to your nugget?"

"No," I said. "It's the lights that talk to me."

"You mean colors? You always have seen colors."

"No, it isn't that." Taking a deep breath, I told him what the voices were telling me. "When I fell, I made a choice to switch places with another soul. That's why nothing seems the same for me. My soul is getting ready for another lesson. I don't even know how to explain that, it is just weird."

"Huh. So, you are getting this information from the voices?"

"Yes."

"Do you think you are seeing real things?" he asked.

"Yes."

"And, the voices? They are not telling you to kill yourself?"

"Hell no!" I exclaimed. "I think they saved me from doing that? Why would I want to do that, John?"

"I don't know. But, that would kill me."

"I know. It would have been selfish of me to leave you to do this by yourself."

"What can I do to help you?"

"Tell me you don't think I am crazy."

"I don't." He kissed me again, "I am here to help you."

"I'll try to remember that when I am going crazy."

John thought this was funny. He laughed for a few minutes. Then, I realized that it was funny and started laughing with him. I was worried about him thinking that I was going crazy and I could still joke about it actually happening. Yes, it was a good thing to have a husband to talk to about this whole head thing. He didn't judge me and took it all in stride.

Chapter 6

Hard Time Regrouping

John's layoff came at one of the hardest times for us. We were never financially stable, but after the layoff, we were relying solely on my income. It wasn't as if he was not looking for something right away, either. On February 2nd, he deferred his student loans, updated his resume with several county websites, and contacted the school for referrals. He spent time every day working on his job hunt. Then, he spent the other half of his day working on my "honey do" list.

The first thing on my list was for him to paint my treatment room at my new studio in the chiropractic clinic. That took a few days, as I could not decide on a color. Of course, it had to be periwinkle, my favorite color. "Why don't you just say purple?" he would ask.

"Because it isn't purple," I would argue. "It is a cross between blue, silver and purple."

"Whatever!" he said, as he rolled his eyes.

Although he was not particularly handy, I believed he could do anything he put his mind to doing. In fact, he once told me that I made him believe he could do anything. I don't know why adults lose faith in our abilities to do anything we put our minds to doing. Regardless, I just kept giving him projects, thinking he could do them. There were days he would clarify what it was I was asking. I asked him to make a sidewalk sign for me. It drove him nuts, but he did a great job on it.

The one thing on my list that really made him irritated was asking him to replace the stabilizer bars on the front end of my Jeep. The parts were $20, but the labor was intensive. We bought the parts in late February. But, it took a month of constant discussion for me to get him to even try doing the job. Working on cars was not his thing. So, how I ever convinced him to do this had to be some type of Divine intervention.

Towards the middle of February, I was sitting home on a Friday night after working. Brooke was at a friend's house, as usual, and it was almost nine p.m. My cellular phone rang and I could see it was John. "Hi," I answered.

"What are you doing?" he asked.

"Sitting here, waiting for you to come home."

"Want to come and get me at the bar?"

"Okay. Why?"

"I want to have a drink and Tom is down here," he said. "Plus, you need to get out for a while and let loose."

"Only one of us can drink, John. I don't think it is going to be me letting loose if you are already having a beer with Tom," I laughed.

"Just come down."

Months before, I had made him promise me to call for a ride, rather than drink and drive. How could I not go down and allow him to have a few drinks when he did what I asked? "Okay, I have to get dressed and will be down shortly."

I took a shower, got dressed and drove down to the bar in Hudson where John was working. We figured out one day that he had worked at the Sports Club for more than 20 years, cooking fish on Friday nights throughout the year. He hunted with the owners, who were like an extension of the Geving family. When I arrived, I parked in the back and walked up the hill to the front of the bar. John gave me his salute from the corner of the bar, where he stood chatting with another man.

As was his habit, he greeted me with a kiss on the lips and a squeeze. "What can I get for you? Tom's buying," he laughed.

"How about just a coke for now?"

John shook his head and said, "You can have a beer, you know? I'm fine."

"I don't want a beer."

"Okay." Then turning to his friend, he introduced me, which is not something the Geving men are known for doing. Introductions were rare with John. He usually just stood there until I introduced myself to his friends. "This is my friend Tom. He was married to Sadie."

Tom shook my hand and told me it was nice to meet me. He was a man of about forty, with curly dark hair and a quick grin. I liked him immediately, and even more as he sat and talked with us. He was funny and easy-going and it made sense that John got along with him.

As I sipped my cola, I participated in the conversation and observed what was going on around me. I noticed my husband rubbing his temples. "What's wrong?" I asked.

"I have a headache," he explained, "and my shoulder is still bothering me." He had been telling me his shoulder was bothering him for two months. In the last week, he said he was just fatigued and found himself sleeping in the middle of the day, while I was at work. I watched as he picked up his new beer on the bar and started to bring the glass to his mouth. His hand was shaking. At the time, I believed it had something to do with the glass being full and his laughing, but he wasn't laughing.

I mention the glass, the headache and the shoulder because these issues persisted for the following month. The other observation that I made that night was his stance. He would lean over the back of a chair, grabbing the sides of it for stability. Then, he would straighten to a full standing position and squeeze his eyes shut, almost like he was dizzy. I asked him if he wanted to sit down twice before he finally decided to do so. I knew there was something wrong because of the lights around him. I couldn't hear the voices over the music and the basketball game on the television and, I was feeling anxious because of the noise.

For John, there had been many nights of closing bars and drinking with friends. In fact, I had closed several bars with John. At 2:30 AM, it was time for us to leave and I was hungry. I needed to eat something, as I had not eaten dinner. "Can you buy breakfast?" I asked John. When he got paid from the Sports Club, he used that money for spending cash. He always had a twenty stuffed in some corner of his wallet.

"Sure. Where do you want to go?"

"How about the truck stop on twelve?" I suggested.

"You and your breakfast thing," he laughed.

"My favorite meal of the day!"

We had our "after the bar" breakfast and headed home about 4:00 A.M. The cat was waiting for us to go to bed and came out to greet us. We undressed and fell into bed, exhausted. The cat climbed up and lay down between my legs and we were out.

The next day, John and I went and bought a new mattress with our tax return. He had been complaining about our bed for months. The mattress was about 7 years old and really needed to be replaced. We both felt that it sucked. We went to lunch at Red Lobster and came home after picking up his car in Hudson. We were pretty tired by the time we got home.

The bed came two weeks later. I was home early one day and John and I were having dinner on the couch, when there was a news story about Natasha Richardson's funeral. She was an actress that was married to another actor named Liam Niesen. She had died March 19, 2009, 3 days after falling and hitting her head while skiing. She had a brain bleed. The sheer coincidence struck me and I turned to John, stating, "That could have been me!"

There was a soft pain in his eyes as he looked at me and said, "I know."

Somehow, this story morphed into a conversation about what we wanted for the other, should one of us die. "I want you to cremate me, Johnny! I don't want anyone looking at my dead body, either," I said.

"OK. I want to be cremated, too."

"Anything in particular for a funeral?"

"Bagpipes," he said, laughing. "I want bagpipes at my funeral. Scatter my ashes at the cabin."

"You realize we would have to have this in the church."

"Yes. Mom needs that."

"But, the Catholic faith does not allow for scattering. You have to stay together."

"No," he shook his head. "You are not burying me in the ground. I'm going to the cabin."

"Don't get me wrong," I assured him, "I don't care if you don't want to be buried in the ground or kept together. I just wanted you to know that having a church service in the Catholic Church will be a pain."

"Well, I don't care. Do you want to be buried?" John said.

"I'm going out in flames. You may not be able to scatter anything." I was laughing a little when I said this.

"No," he shook his head. "I'm going first."

"What?" I asked. "No, you aren't." Then, after stewing about this for a minute, I asked him, "Will you remarry? I think you should remarry."

"No! I won't remarry. But, you will. You need to promise me," he said. "If I die before you, please promise me to remarry."

"Why wouldn't you remarry?"

He looked at me like I had two heads. "If I lose you, I will not have anything to give someone else. You will take me with you, but I won't know where we went. I will be gone for a long time without you. You, on the other hand, need people."

"You need people, too."

"Promise me you will remarry after I die."

"That isn't entirely up to me, John! I have to meet someone who would be willing to put up with my shit for a long time. I will not go through the death of a spouse twice in my lifetime."

"You will meet someone. You will marry again."

"How can you be so sure?" I asked.

"You need people," he stated again. "You need someone to love you and keep you grounded."

He was right. I knew that John was my grounding post. He was Brooke's, too. If we lost him, she and I would bounce off of each other like positive charges, zapping each other with an arc of energy that would scorch us.

Somehow, he extracted a promise from me. Then, I extracted a promise from him. If he died before I did, he would do everything within his spiritual power to send the right person to me and help me to recognize him. If I had known then how pissed off this promise would make me, I would have never made it in the first place. But, I did and he made a similar one.

Looking back, I wonder at the knowledge we had. As with most married couples, I think there was a connection on a soul level. We knew that our souls called out to each other and came together as one. Yet, how did that work when the other half of the soul, which belongs to your spouse when you marry, dies? Most Christian faiths believe that you make a covenant with God and your spouse to love until you are parted by death. However, once these souls became entwined, how can you separate them without breaking the whole? That soul would be ripped in half and shredded. On that day in March, we both had this understanding. We both knew that if one of us died, the other would need a push. John insisted that he would not remarry. I insisted that I was going first. Yet, we both knew that we would support the other, regardless of who went first.

Brooke was there for some of our conversation. I think she actually walked in on the end of it, when we were discussing remarriage. She was uncomfortable and went into her room, stating that she didn't want to hear it. Though, she did say that she wanted "Somewhere Over the Rainbow" sang at the funeral. John nodded. He sang that song to her when she was down. That was one of their things. They had many things together. I could never fill in for him if he was gone. He remembered every memory. Her first steps, her first words, her thinking, her mother, her history, etc. I knew only what I was told.

The noise in the room was becoming too loud for me. I told John I needed to relax. I did not have any clients for massage that day, so I did not have to go in. He asked what we were having for dinner and I said, 'Peanut butter and jelly sandwiches, if you don't think of anything else."

A loud, resounding "ICK!" came from Brooke's bedroom.

"You and Brooke decide. I'm not in the mood to cook." I needed to lie down, as I knew that they were both going to ask me to decide on dinner. Neither one of them could make a decision without having some input from someone else. I wasn't about to tell them what to fix, as I was the only one in the house at the time that worked full time, had a part-time job, and a head injury. I couldn't handle sound because there was so much of it in my head. I could not see straight most days because of the dizziness. Also, I could not see anything but spots. I needed to lie down for a few minutes.

A couple days after the conversation about our funerals, John's brother, Dan, and his wife, Renee, went into labor with their second child. There were complications with the delivery and the child was stillborn. We both hurt for them. Although we could not have children, we had two miscarriages before I found out there was really no hope of me ever carrying a baby full term. The pain of losing any child, baby or fetus, resonates with many men and women. When we found out about the death of Tyler, we knew and felt the pain for his parents, Dan and Renee.

They scheduled a memorial service for the baby in Menomonie, where they were living, the following Thursday. John was going to paint at his mom's that day and agreed to meet me and Brooke at the ride share, so we could go together. That week, John and I had switched cars so that he could finally fix the stabilization bars on my Jeep. I was excited to be able to drive it again, as his Cherokee was too awkward for me. There was something about it that just did not fit me like my Wrangler did.

On that Tuesday, before the memorial service, I was pulled over by New Richmond Police because, I was told, the license plate was dirty. There had to be another reason for him pulling me over, but the officer did not give me any other reason. I explained that it was my husband's car and cooperated with him. My record was clean, so when he ran his little check on my license, he found nothing. When I asked John about what they wanted with him, he laughed and said, "You were driving. They obviously have an issue with you running stop lights in town."

"I haven't run a stoplight in a long time!" I argued.

Rolling his eyes and sighing, he was opening his mouth to say something, when Brooke's voice piped up from her bedroom, "Ha! You ran a red light with me last week!"

John began to laugh. "Dear, you don't even realize how many lights you run. You need to pay attention. I worry

71

about you driving because you are so preoccupied with the voices in your head right now."

"Don't say that to me!" I was offended by what he was implying here. "You know darn well that I am not crazy!"

"I didn't say that," he sighed. "I think that you have so much going on that you need to process that you forget you are driving. Ask them," he waved his arms around in circles to indicate the lights and spirits around him, "to leave you alone while you are driving! Or, ask them to keep you safe."

I realized that it was me that assumed I was crazy because I had been hearing more voices and seeing more lights around since my head injury. I knew that these things were higher level energies that communicated, but I did not understand everything yet. I did not understand how I was supposed to work with this stuff I was seeing. "You are right. I don't always notice the light is red."

"And," he laughed, "You don't always notice it is green either. You have stopped at green lights and floored it through red. Just promise me that you will pay more attention to the colors of the stoplights than the ones in the car with you!"

"I promise. No more red lights."

"I'm going to go look at that license plate. I think the cop just wanted a reason to stop you." It was determined that the cop did stop me for another reason, as both John and

I could see the license plate just fine. "Yeah, I am using only one eye and can tell he was stopping you for another reason entirely."

"Well, I need to go massage," I told him. "Can I take my car?"

"No," he said. "I have something to finish before it can be driven."

Due to the continual dizziness from my head injury, the chiropractor I worked with was doing this odd adjustment that required him to hold my head and reposition it. Then, I stood up with him holding my head. Typically, this worked for about 2-4 days, or until I put my arms above my head for a period of time. As a massage therapist, we are always bending, putting our arms above our head and turning with movement. He gave me an adjustment at least once a week, if not more.

John had painted my treatment room and put up shelves that we had bought from the chiropractor, Dr. Leo. John had made my sidewalk sign and I had put a business sign with specials in it. My work presence was moving forward. The doctor and I were getting used to each other in our new space and learning what the other person knew. Somewhere along this path, we were developing a mutual respect for each other's healing modalities. Now, if only I could get John over to paint the walls in the back room after he was done at his mom's. However, he was getting sick of painting and kept complaining about his shoulder hurting.

"I'm just beat!" he would say.

He used to take cat naps. Twenty minutes lying down and he was good. Every so often, I would see him leaning over a chair, holding the back like he was trying to steady himself. I would ask him what was wrong and he would tell me his shoulder hurt and he was trying to stretch it. I knew there was something more. "If that doesn't go away in a couple days, I want you to make an appointment with the doctor," I told him.

"I'm fine."

I gave him "the look" that he and his daughter insist that I have. "It's time you go in for a physical anyway."

"No."

At some point, I just sighed at him and walked away. He was as stubborn about going to the doctor, or dentist, as most men were. He just refused to get checked. He would troop out to the garage, do his weight training and stationary bike, then, come in and ask what we were having for dinner. I told him, "Whatever you are making, as I don't want to have to cook after working a 12-15 hour day!"

Thursday came and John and I made arrangements to meet at the park and ride in Roberts after work so that we could go to the memorial service for his nephew. John was going to pick up Brooke and we were all going to drive together. After the service, we were meeting my friend Tara and her son, Jo, at a pizza place in Menomonie. Jo was 14 and he had a crush on Brooke, as she did him. Tara and John had no issue with them pursuing the crush, but I did. Brooke was 17 and would be 18 in June. I understood that age differences in relationships did not matter in the long run, but in the early years it did.

We went to the memorial service and spent a couple hours paying our respects. Then, we went to Ted's Pizza and split a pizza with Tara and the kids. On the way home, we got into a discussion with Brooke about Jo. It was not all together pleasant for me, as I heard all of the warnings and noise in my head. John kept saying, "I don't see the problem, if Tara is alright with it." In the end, I was still opposed, but resigned to the fact that it wasn't up to me.

John went to bed. Brooke went to bed. I washed my face and played online for about an hour before going to bed. When I got into bed on my side, John rolled over and gave me a kiss. As I still had an overactive mind, I asked him a question that I had asked him several times before, "Why are you so opposed to adoption?"

He let out a frustrated sigh and abruptly said, "I don't know!" Then, he rolled over to face away from me. It was a direct rejection that I had not felt from him. It hurt. Yet, I did not react the way I would have before my head injury. Before my head injury, I would have cried and rolled away from him too. Instead, I said, "Well, I'm sorry you feel that way. I'll be bringing it up again."

"Could you not do it when we are going to bed?" he asked. "We can't have a discussion about that right now."

"Fine! Sorry I brought it up."

Even though I felt hurt, I let it go and went to sleep. I had to work the next day and my energy was off-balance. I awoke most days feeling depleted and went to bed feeling like I could go all night. It just didn't seem right. But, I realized that thinking about this topic of adoption all night was not going to resolve my husband's feelings. I let it go.

Chapter 7

Endings That Start Something

Friday, March twenty-seventh, started like every other day since John was laid off. I got up, took my shower, told him I loved him, gave him a kiss, and left for work. I knew he would sleep a bit longer and get up, do his workout, look for jobs online, and then do whatever else was on his "honey do" list. Since he had mentioned having headaches and a sore shoulder several times for over a month, I did not want to wake him that morning. He looked like he was sleeping so peacefully. I bent over and kissed his head, whispering, "I love you," into his ear.

He turned over and presented his lips with a sleepy smile. "I love you, too!"

"Go back to sleep," I told him. "It's early."

"I will. I'm going to my mom's to paint today and then, to the Sports Club."

"Okay. You have a good day," I told him, kissing him on the mouth.

"You, too. I love you."

"I love you, too." I wanted so much to crawl back into bed with him. But, one of us had to work. After my head injury, I had limited vacation time available and I was taking a trip to Houston the next Wednesday to celebrate my friend Stacey's 40th birthday. John had encouraged me to book the ticket that week, even though I was having issues remembering her. But, I knew she was important to me. John had told me she was my maid of honor in our wedding and had been like a sister to me in college.

So, off to a fun-filled day in the call center I went! I hated my job, which I remembered while teaching myself how to do it again. The company did not want to expend their resources to retrain me, as I was one of the trainers of certain subject matter. At the time, I felt it was just their way of getting rid of me without taking responsibility. At least, that was what my suspicions were. I was starting to remember more of what made me fabulous at my work. People yelled at me and I didn't yell back. I just explained to them what I could and could not do for them. I helped the customer service representatives with procedures and policies and kept my supervisor from actually having to do anything. Yes, what a fun day I had in store for me! But, it was Friday, and I had vacation next week!

As I walked out of the bedroom, the lights that I was seeing on a regular basis started moving around me. The voices I heard kicked up and told me to go back into the bedroom and give John another kiss. One distinct voice urged gently, "Toni, you need to go back in and kiss him again!" For the first time since this change, I actually did what I was being told. I went back into the bedroom and kissed him.

"I thought you had left?" he said sleepily.

"Almost," I smiled. "I had to come back to kiss you again."

"Aren't you going to be late?"

"No," I said. "I have time."

As I turned to go, there was a beautiful angel standing next to me. She smiled and told me that everything would be fine. She told me to go to work. At the time, I felt that these were just hallucinations that were brought on by my head injury. I had seen ghosts before and had dreams of angels and people who had passed, but never had I seen angels in front of me. Colors and lights, I had seen. Actual beings standing in front of me were beyond anything I would have expected. But, her calm reassurance made me feel like the day would be good.

The day was busy and I had some time to talk to John on my lunch, but he was at his mom's painting the inside of her trailer. The weather was unseasonably warm for March. I walked around the office building outside with short sleeves, which was almost too cold. But, wearing a jacket was too warm. The snow and sub-zero temperatures had gone after St. Patrick's Day. During the day, it was in the mid- sixty degree temperatures.

When I got home, I needed to change clothes and get to the chiropractic office. Even though I was running late, I thought I should call John. I was looking at the clock on our kitchen wall and taking off my wedding band, as I always did before leaving the house. It was 5:11 P.M., so John was already at work at the bar. The angel that was there this morning was gone, but there were others that were hanging around me as I went out the door, heading to my massage studio. They felt like a cushion around me. It was comforting in a way, and somewhat disconcerting.

Since my sidewalk incident, I had been getting adjustments from the chiropractic doctor for my neck pain and dizziness. The vertigo would go away for a couple days, until I raised my hands above my head, or looked up. I told him that I was getting dizziness again. "You know, Toni," Doctor Leo said, "if you would give yourself a week off, this treatment might help for more than a day."

"Maybe I will when John gets a job," I laughed.

After the adjustment, I was done for the day and heading home. I had nothing on my schedule until the following Monday. So, I promised I would take the weekend to keep my arms below my head and try not to look up. "Try doing it for a week," he advised as I packed up my bag.

As I was leaving the clinic, I could not help but notice that emergency vehicle sirens were going off every few minutes. Doctor Leo wondered what was going on that the sirens were going so much. I had been wondering the same thing.

When I got home about ten minutes before seven, I was overwhelmed by the sirens and the lack of whispering. I went into the apartment in my short sleeves hungry. I was looking for something to eat and Brooke started pushing the noodle salad she had made in home economics, telling me it was "AMAZING!" I told her to dish me up some of her salad while I went to get into something comfortable to watch my Friday night show, "The Ghost Whisperer". John would be working late because it was two weeks before Easter, and the bar would be busy with their Friday night fish fry. The Sports Club served all-you-could-eat perch and cod every Friday and were especially busy during Lent.

I changed out of my scrubs into sweatpants and a t-shirt. "Can we turn off the lights and close the drapes?" I asked. "I just don't want to deal with anyone tonight."

"Sure," Brooke laughed. She gave me a plate of her salad and I admitted it was very good. I was on the second bite when we realized our show was not on and the March Madness College basketball tournament was starting. Seconds after this disappointing realization, the doorbell rang.

"Will you get that please?" I asked her.

"Yes." She looked out the window next to the door and then opened the door. After exchanging a few words, I heard her say, "Just a minute." Then, she turned to me and said that I needed to come to the door.

I will never forget the look on her face. It was a cross between total panic and complete anxiety. Though, I didn't register it at the time. I was annoyed that I had to come to the door. She whispered to me as I passed her that it was a police officer outside. So, I opened the door to see a New Richmond police officer in his black uniform standing there, looking like there were a million other places he wanted to be.

"Yes?" I said to the man who had to be 10 years younger than I.

"Are you Toni Geving?"

"Yes."

"Are you related to John Geving?"

"My husband is John Geving."

"Does he live here with you?"

"Yes."

"Is there another John Geving?"

"Yes," I knew this wasn't good. "My father-in-law is also John Geving, but he goes by Jack."

"Do you mind if I come in?"

"No." I opened the door and admitted the officer. I saw Brooke with her knees to her chest, sitting in one of the recliner chairs, rocking back and forth like she had a mental condition. She watched with the same panicked- anxious expression on her face. "Could you turn off the television?" I asked her. She did.

I sat down in the other chair, indicating to the officer that he may sit. But, he stood there, in front of Johnny's buck mount and musky, facing me. He started asking questions about John. How old was he? Did he have any medical conditions? Where was he today? What was he doing? I was getting a clue that something was seriously wrong, and so was Brooke. The lights in the room had stopped flashing and seemed to stand still. The voices stopped chatting. The only noise was Brooke's stupid ring tone that grated on my nerves- something singing about being horny.

I felt calm. I had this feeling like I should be reacting differently to a police officer standing in my living room, asking me questions about my husband. Was he a diabetic? Did he have any heart condition? Does he text and drive? The questions were meant to uncover something. My nerves were frazzled. Then, Brooke's horny phone sounded again. I wanted to tell her to shut her fucking ring tone off, but I was trying to focus my attention on the officer. At some point, I said, "Just tell me what this is about."

And, he did.

"Mrs. Geving, at approximately 5:11 this evening, John Geving was in a car accident and it was fatal. He crossed the center line and was killed when his car crashed into another oncoming vehicle."

"What?" I asked, looking at Brooke as she cried and rocked next to me.

I wanted to cry, too. But I couldn't. I didn't know what to do first. So, I said, "Brooke, it's OK."

She looked at me like I had 4 heads. I know I probably did at that point. I just could not seem to think. I heard the officer say, "Is there anyone that can come sit with you until the medical examiner gets here?"

"Um..." I was thinking of my father-in-law, the most even- keeled guy I knew. But, I would have to tell him that his eldest son was gone. "Yes, I have to find my phone. I'll call Jack."

"I'll wait until he gets here."

Brooke's phone rang and I lost it. "Please take that in your room! Turn off your ringer! And don't say anything to anyone until I get a hold of family." I couldn't help it. The ring tone and the lack of noise, when that is all I'd been hearing for months, were making me panic now. I was looking for my phone and trying to figure out the number for my father-in-law's phone. Just as I found it, Brooke came in and shoved her phone in my face. "I can't! It's Grandma!" she yelled at me.

All I could think was, "Oh God! I have to tell them both?"

"Hi Ann," I said quietly.

"What's wrong with Brooke?" she yelled into the phone. Brooke was hysterically sobbing.

Instead of answering her question, I asked, "Where are you?"

"I'm at home. Why?"

"Is anyone there with you?"

"No. What's wrong with Brooke?"

Ignoring her questions, I kept asking my own. "Where is Jeff? Is he still there?"

"No. He left."

"I need you to call him and have him come back and get you."

"Why? What's wrong with Brooke?"

I think I sighed. "Ann, please listen to me. John was in an accident tonight and it was fatal. I have a police officer here waiting for me to call Jack to come here."

"What? When? Johnny's okay, right?"

"No, Ann. I'm sorry. He was killed in a car accident. It was fatal." I said as calmly as I could. Inside, I felt the twisting of my stomach and knew I wasn't eating the rest of my noodle salad. "I need to call Jack. But, I want you to call Jeff and have him come back to get you."

"What?"

"Ann, I have to go now. The medical examiner will be here by nine." I believe I hung up on her. Just disconnected the phone and handed it back to Brooke, who was angrily sobbing and pacing. Then, I couldn't remember what I was going to do. Oh yeah, I was calling Jack.

As if I needed to, I turned to the policeman and said, "I'm sorry. That was his mother. I never thought I would have to tell his parents that he was dead."

Somehow, I found the number in my phone and called Shari, Jack's wife. When she answered, I asked to speak with Jack. She handed her phone to him and I heard the familiar, "Hello?"

"Jack, are you home now?"

"Yes."

"Is there any way you can come here?"

"Yes, what's wrong?"

"John was in an accident tonight and the police officer will not leave until someone is here with us. It was a fatal accident Jack. Johnny is gone."

"We'll be there in about 20 minutes."

"Thank you."

To this day, I don't know what his parents felt when I told them. I can't imagine that the sinking feeling that I felt days later was the same as anything they had. This was their oldest son and I felt like I just wiped him off the earth for them. I don't even know if I was gentle enough in telling them. All I know is that I was not able to think. I had to call my mom. I had to have someone there just for me. I needed people that could be supportive of my grieving process and not expect me to support them in return.

Shari and Jack came in my door about 20 minutes later and the police officer left me his card and explained that the medical examiner would be here later. As I was letting the police officer out, there were friends of the Geving's coming up the walk. I just shook my head and asked them to come back. I needed a few minutes. I wanted a few hours- days, to just process this. But, I didn't have it and I knew it. Jack and Shari were not there for more than 5 minutes when I realized, "I have to call the Sport's Club. They are expecting John and he is already three hours late!"

"I'll call them," Shari said.

I called my mom while she did that. I don't remember exactly what I said to her, but she explained later that I had told her John was in an accident and when she asked if he was all right, I told her, "No, he's dead." I was told that I said it without emotion. I still wasn't feeling anything- just numbness. I felt this odd acceptance that I was going to do this life thing alone for some time.

I talked to my friend Tara, and left two messages for my good friend, Cally. I knew she was out with her brother, so I had to wait for her to call back. Tara promised to come the next day. She had seen the accident report on the news. That night was clear and warm. There was no snow on the roads and the ice had melted. However, there were 5 fatal accidents that night. John's was the third fatal accident in the county for the year. This explained all of the sirens.

As I suspected, the next people in the door were Jeff and Ann. Later, several of the childhood friends came through the door. The medical examiner had not arrived yet. Everyone had a phone with a stupid ring tone. Everyone was talking. My cell started buzzing, because I was the only one that turned my phone on vibrate. Then, the home phone started ringing. I had to find a quiet place to talk and couldn't. I wanted everyone who was not family to leave. But, I couldn't be rude. At about 9:30, Dr. Leo called me. He had received a call from Debbie, one of John's aunts, telling the news. Somehow, news traveled to the ends of New Richmond and beyond in a matter of hours.

I told Jeff to call John's friends from school and Bill, who lived next door. "I can't tell him," I said out loud.

"I will," Jack assured me.

Cally called me back while she was driving. "I need you to pull over," I told her.

"I'm not drinking."

"I need you to pull over because I don't want you to lose signal while I am talking to you, and I don't want you driving."

I could hear gravel as she hit the shoulder of the road. "Okay, I stopped," she said. "What's wrong?"

"Cheetos was in an accident tonight and it was fatal."

"What?"

"I am waiting for the medical examiner to get here."

"Where did this happen?"

"He was on 128 going south towards Cady."

"Oh my God!"

I could hear her brother asking her what was wrong, repeatedly. "He's gone and I can't do anything about it."

"Do you want me to come?" she asked.

"I will need you here tomorrow," I told her. She said she would be at my house in the afternoon on Saturday. It was in talking to her that I realized that I was feeling overwhelmed and helpless. I knew she would be able to see his spirit there with me, while I was not able to then. Somehow, I knew she would help me. But, I wouldn't need her until the next day.

As I hung up with her, I turned around thinking that I wished these people would 'get the fuck out of my house.' They were just making noise and not helping the situation at all. Not one of them really acknowledged me when they came in; they just started socializing in my kitchen and were there for the Geving's. My apartment was a mess. The noise was more overwhelming than any of the whispering I had been hearing for months. I believed it was because the noise these visitors were making held no meaning for me. Even after asking them to turn their phones on vibrate, their phones continued to disrupt my ability to understand anything going on around me. What did I have to say to make them understand I could not handle their noise?

When the medical examiner showed up, it was close to 10:00 P.M. She came in with a bag of John's belongings. His wallet, minus his driver's license, and some other miscellaneous things he had on him. The wallet had his blood on it and was sealed in a bag. She came in and I told her that I was John's wife. Brooke was taking the seat next to me and began rocking and crying again. I knew she was thinking about her dad not being there for her graduation, her birthday, her wedding, her children, her support, etc. Her dad was her everything, as he was mine. Yet, I needed to hear what the medical examiner had to say and was not able to help Brooke at that time. Even if I could, she was not ready to accept help from me.

The examiner told me her name was Patty. She gave me her whole name, but I clung to Patty because it was easy. She explained that she was called to the accident at approximately 5:15 and after John's vehicle had crossed the center line, bypassing a vehicle, sideswiping a second vehicle and coming to a stop in a head on collision. When she was able to get into the car, he had a coffee cup between his legs and had been killed on impact. She explained that the driver in the car he was in a front end collision with was air lifted to Regions, where he was reported in stable, but serious condition. There were no other injuries in the accident.

She asked the same questions about John's health. Did he have any medical conditions? Did he have any heart problems or seizures? Was he diabetic? One of the witnesses stated he appeared to be slumped over the wheel or reaching for something. He was pronounced dead at the scene. She had given me the bag with his wallet, which I had set between myself and Brooke. Brooke asked if she could open it and I asked her to wait. However, the medical examiner nodded and she tore open the bag and took the wallet. She rifled through the contents looking for a picture of her, as her dad always carried one. "Where is my picture?" she cried.

"He had it in the console," I explained, knowing the picture was there.

Patty asked if I had any questions she could answer.

Brooke said, before I could answer, "I do."

I knew exactly what she was going to ask, as the angels were telling me, "He did not suffer."

"Brooke," I started to say, "don't go there."

"Did he suffer?" she asked.

Patty got up to hug her and whisper to her, while I came under attack from her uncle, my brother-in-law, Jeff. "Don't you lie to her! She has a right to know!" he yelled at me.

"Jeff, I wasn't-"

"Shut up! She has more of a right to be here than you. She's his blood! You're not!" he yelled at me.

"I'm his wife!" I said as calmly as I could, but still raised my voice.

"Stop fighting!" Brooke yelled.

It was Jack who stepped in between Jeff and me, pulling him out of the room. I was so hurt, angry and confused that I just stared at him. It was Patty who told Brooke she could have his wallet and took me out of the equation completely. It was Jeff who gave Brooke the permission to walk all over me and treat me like shit for the next year. He endorsed her importance over mine. Though, it would be me who would have the legal responsibility of everything to come. I swallowed all of the things I wanted to say and just internalized the hurt and pain, knowing that I was going to have to always stand for John because I didn't matter here.

When the medical examiner left, Julie and Todd came in the door. Shortly after that, my mom, brother and two sisters came. I think they were there within an hour and a half of me calling my mom. It was after 10. Jill and Tom came in after that, as they were in Madison for Michael's wrestling tournament. Jeff, Julie, and Jill were John's younger triplet siblings. I don't remember when I asked the question, but I specifically remember asking Ann and Jeff before the medical examiner got there if John had been drinking.

Ann's response was, "He had one or two."

Jeff's response was, "Yes, he had a few."

I asked if he should have been driving and they both gave me answers that were vague. Jeff said he was fine. Ann didn't say anything. I knew there was more than either was telling me, as the whispering was gently telling me the truth. "He had been drinking and it was more than he should have been."

The message I kept hearing from one of the voices was "prepare for the worst and expect the best. We will protect you." However, these whispers were hard to discern amidst all the other noises. My family was there for me and Brooke. It was nice to see them, as they could relate to both of us. My mom knew what it was like to lose a spouse in her early 40's. My siblings knew what it was to lose a father as a young child or adult. Although Brooke knew that, she refused to think anyone could identify with her loss. As most young adults and children, she could not see that pain was pain. I knew that my experience was different than my mother's, but the pain of John's death did not hurt more or less than what she felt. I was just in a different place than she was.

I do not remember what time Bill, John's friend, arrived. However, I knew it was after the medical examiner had left and my confrontation with Jeff. He came in the door and was looking at all the people in my apartment. As he stood there, I saw Jack go over and place his hands on Bill's shoulders. I could not hear what he said, but I could see the tears start as he looked at me and listened. John was loved by many people and he had some great friends from school. As this one absorbed the shock of losing his best friend, who was like a brother, I felt the need to comfort him. He came to me and I gave him a hug. "I'm sorry Toni! I can't believe this," he said to me.

"Neither can I."

"Are you okay?" he asked.

I don't remember what I said, but I remember it was close to, "Ask me tomorrow." I was still in shock and still wanted everyone to leave. Though, I knew if they did, I would have to think. Eventually, I would start to feel through the numbness. I would have to start processing the information and absorb the shock of losing my other half. The tears would have to come. I knew that I was not ready to fall apart when John wasn't there to pick up the pieces.

Chapter 8

Just Go Home

It was well after midnight before everyone left my apartment. My mom and siblings left around 12:30 AM. Jack and Shari had left earlier, probably for the same reason I wanted everyone to leave- the noise and closeness of everyone. There were several times that I wanted to stand up and scream for everyone to leave. But, I did not want to draw any more attention to myself. I didn't want anyone to know how close I was to losing even more of my mind and self-control. Although I was not ready to cry, I certainly was not ready to give up on the idea that I was in a very bad nightmare.

Every time the door to the apartment opened that night, and for months after that, I expected John to walk through the door. I had it in my mind that he would come in, do his little salute that he gave when he entered a room full of friends and family, and ask me why I didn't tell him I was having a party. He would wonder where the beer was, much like his brother had asked at some point that evening. But, I knew it wasn't a dream.

As I turned off the outside light and locked my front door, I finally heard the silence. There was no sound, or movement. Brooke was standing there watching me, as I stood in the middle of the living room. "I don't think I am going to sleep," she said, with fresh tears forming in her eyes. I took her into my arms and told her that we both had to try. It was either that, or cleaning the apartment, which just did not sound like what I needed at 2:00 AM. We agreed that neither one of us wanted to do any cleaning. Somehow, I convinced her to try and sleep, stating that I was going to do the same.

When I went into the bedroom, I noticed the cat was curled up in a ball of black fur on John's side of the bed. Nova had hid in our bedroom when the police officer came and did not come out until everyone left. He looked up at me and yawned, stretching his legs before coming over to rub against me. He seemed to understand I needed to cuddle. Animals were great at sensing emotions. This cat knew all of us well, regularly giving us his attention and intuitive energy work. He had been spending the days on John's lap when he was sitting watching television. I cuddled with him for a few minutes until he left the room, looking for John. It wasn't long when he came back into the room, meowing like he was asking a question. It sounded sad. His big green eyes questioned mine, and then he butted his head against my arm.

"I know," I whispered. "I want him here, too."

For about twenty minutes, I tried to shut my mind off and sleep. I lay down and the bed began to spin like I had drunk too much. If I hadn't received the positioning treatment from Dr. Leo, I would have thought it was vertigo. But, there was nausea associated with it. As all I had to eat was the two bites of Brooke's noodle salad and water, I was hoping the nausea would pass. I wasn't even hungry.

As I laid there in the darkness, I saw the lights floating around and tried to ask for answers. Although the voices had gone quiet, I knew they were there. Was it just that I could not hear them? Or, had they finally shut up? The angel that had encouraged me to go back and give John another kiss good-bye was there somewhere. I could not see her, but I felt her. "Why didn't you tell me it would be the last time I saw him?" I thought to myself. I remember feeling someone touch me and a weight sitting on the bed next to me. The touch was soft, but I felt it.

I physically ached in my chest because it wasn't John. He wasn't coming into bed late and kissing me on the cheek to tell me he loved me.

I gave up trying to sleep and booted up my laptop. I went on Facebook to find that someone had already posted condolences to my wall. What a way to find out about John's passing! I hope that most of the family was notified before this. What do I say to these people that were spreading my bad news for me? Who started this mess? How was I going to deal with this very public way of spreading the bad news?

At some point, as I mindlessly played a game, I started to pray. Not a prayer that begged God to stop this cruel joke, but a real prayer for John and the other people involved in the accident. "Please Lord, send your angels to help John pass into Heaven and allow his sins to be forgiven. Help the other people involved to recover from this trauma and be healthy, especially the man airlifted to Regions. Please help me to be strong for Brooke and everyone. And, if Johnny is actually in some Witness Protection program and didn't take us, please allow us to see him again someday- if for no other reason, but to kick his ass."

The only reason I thought about the whole Witness Protection Program was because John and I were addicted to a television show on USA called *In Plain Sight.* The story line was about U.S. Marshals that were assigned to the Witness Protection Program in New Mexico. We loved it! However far-fetched the idea of John witnessing a crime that potentially endangered his life, and that of his family, without him telling me, I hoped that by some weird Wisconsin law, he was required to hide out without us. At least, he would be alive.

At some point, I logged off my computer and lay down with my head pressed up against John's pillow. I fell into a fitful sleep for a couple hours. It was around 5:30 when I started cleaning my living room, pushing all the crap into my bedroom. Some of the stuff in the boxes was thrown away. Some of it was put into a pile. I dusted when Brooke got up. I asked her to straighten her room up. I cleaned off the kitchen table, swept the floor and wiped up the counters. We now had room for people to sit on the couches and place food on the table. "Isn't that what people do when their friends were grieving?" I thought. "Don't they bring food?"

By six o'clock that morning, I needed a shower. I knew people would start coming over early and that John's family would be there to hear what I had to say about the funeral. I had to make an appointment to meet with the funeral director the next day, as the medical examiner had asked which funeral home to send the body to the night before. I referred to the family for guidance, as I didn't know there was more than one in New Richmond. Evidently, people chose the funeral home based on where the services would be. As John and I had both been raised in the Catholic faith, I was told to use Cullen's funeral home, across from the Methodist Church. So, that is where John's body was going.

Brooke had helped me with some of the cleaning. I asked her to vacuum the living room while I showered and cleaned up the bathroom. Neither one of us had slept more than a couple hours. Brooke was still red-eyed from crying. I had not shed more than a couple tears. I couldn't break down yet. When I did, I did not know that my crying would stop. I didn't want Brooke to see me cry. I didn't want anyone to see me cry. I just wanted to process this and give myself time later, when I was alone.

It was the shower that did me in! Brooke was playing music loud enough to be heard over the vacuum cleaner. Even if my neighbors were not happy that some band was blaring at 6:30 in the morning on a Saturday, I decided it was not a big deal. As I stepped into the heat of the shower spray, I began to sob. Water spraying on my face and chest, the tightness that caused my head and shoulders to throb in pain started to open the floodgate for my eyes. The anguished sounds coming from my mouth were muted by the shower spray, the music and the vacuum. I felt the bile rise from my stomach and I vomited this acidic, clear liquid onto the bath tub floor. Leaning into the spray with my hands on the wall, I tried to just let go and allow the shower to wash away whatever it could.

At some point, I started to pray again. This time, my prayers were for answers. "Why him? Why Him? Why not me? How am I supposed to help Brooke? She needed him! God, why do I have to be the one to go through this pain?" I didn't understand why it was me that was still there. I was the one who hit my head. Why was I still here? I was still sobbing and trying to stay on my feet. I hadn't eaten anything but two bites of noodle salad and water since the night before. I wasn't hungry, but I was physically and emotionally wrecked. I hurt everywhere in my body and mind.

I realized that I needed to sit down when I heard a rushing sound in my ears, like right before one passes out. I became cold in the heat of the shower and decided it was time to shut it off. Wrapping a towel around my body, I sat town on the edge of the tub and breathed through the remaining tears. I didn't want Brooke to know I was crying. I didn't want to face the family with tears. I didn't want to face my life without John. It seemed so unfair. So, I took my time drying off and collecting myself. When I was ready, I exited the bathroom, went into my bedroom and dressed. "You may want to wait for some hot water," I said to Brooke as I came out of the bathroom.

As I dressed, the light beings I was seeing on a regular basis started lighting up to full beam. Then, the whispering amplified and meshed like a thousand people talking in a sacred place, where whispering is expected. All I could think was "here I go again."

"Brooke," I called from the bedroom, "I don't want to hear your fucking ring tone today. Please turn your phone on vibrate."

She didn't like me saying that, but she did do it. I turned my cell phone on vibrate, too. Then, I turned the ringer on the house phone down to a 4. Later, I would change the voice mail message and turn the ringer off, as the phone ringing grated on me. But, I didn't think of that until someone suggested it on Sunday or Monday. It was so much easier to call people back.

At some point after my shower, I received a call from someone asking if they could stop by with some food. I was eating a piece of toast with strawberry jam on it. Why shouldn't someone stop by with food at 7:00 AM on a Saturday morning? We all needed to eat. So, she brought these chocolate peanut butter brownies and something else. The brownies were so good that I don't even remember what else she brought. A serious addiction was developed to these things and, though I tried, I never received the recipe. I was sure I would need treatment someday for these things. I almost hid the pan for myself.

My husband's family started showing up sometime after 8. I remember that it was a beautiful day. The sky was clear and the temperature was a mild 53 degrees. It felt more like May than March. I learned quickly that one of the grieving rituals really was to bring food. Someone brought some frosted brownies and other types of pan cookies. My sister-in-law sent a couple casseroles with my brother, Bruce, and my mom. She also made a bunch of sandwiches on dinner buns with ham, turkey and cheese. Someone brought Subway sandwiches that were cut in quarters and soda. There was a Jell-O™ salad with marshmallows, a vegetable tray with dip and fruit.

If people were not hauling a tray of some sort, they were cleaning my kitchen, my walk, my bathroom. Someone actually ran and got toilet paper and tissues. I watched John's Aunt Debby sweeping my walk and my kitchen floor and wondered, "Why the hell did I clean this morning? It looks like I didn't do shit!"

Again, the people coming in did not understand that I really meant it when I asked them to turn their ringers off on their phones. Then, when my home phone rang, either Brooke or I had to answer it. At one point, I heard Brooke say, "Look you ass, my dad just died and we really don't need you calling asking about our car insurance." Then, she burst into tears and went in her room. I decided that it should probably be my responsibility to answer the phone.

I realized that I needed to call our insurance company and start a claim for John's accident. I remember thinking that somehow the accident had to be reported by someone already, right? I mean, didn't the police have all his insurance information from the glove box? Or, did I really need to call in a claim? All he had was liability insurance on his vehicle.

When my father-in-law got there, I told him I had some phone calls to make and asked him to play host to the many self-invited guests. That's what it felt like for me. These people created a party because my husband had died, then, decided to have it at my house and force me to host it. I didn't want to host this party! And, if I had to be at this party, I didn't want to be sober.

I called the claims department for my insurance company and explained that I needed to report an accident that happened the night before involving my husband and his vehicle. I remember telling the woman who answered the phone that I wasn't sure how to do it and found myself trying to soften the news that John had been killed. I wasn't sure if that was for me or her. But, when I got to the part that he was killed, I started to cry a little. I told her what I knew and asked her to get a police report for the details. She told me about the benefits and said that the State of Wisconsin had a medical benefit for injury or death on liability. She explained the limitations of the policy and the maximum $300,000 provision. "With liability only, the policy will pay up to $100,000 per person to a maximum of $300,000."

"So, the other people involved will have that from our policy?" I questioned.

"Yes."

"Could you find out if the man airlifted to Regions made it? I just need to have peace with that. I don't want to believe this accident caused two deaths."

"I will try to pull the reports and will be talking to all involved parties."

She gave me a claim number, which I wrote down somewhere on a clipboard of crap that I pulled to keep organized with all the death stuff. Sometime during the day, I misplaced it, only to find it on the table in the kitchen where I had set it, looked at it, and ignored it for hours. I thanked her and she expressed that she was sorry for my loss. Having worked in insurance for 8 years, I almost complimented her on her use of empathy without responsibility. Her boss would be proud that she never committed to paying anything on the claim.

With my cordless home phone in hand, I walked outside and to the end of the sidewalk. I wanted to smoke a cigarette. Although I wasn't a regular smoker, I needed something to do with my hands. John chewed tobacco and I smoked occasionally. I was walking down the driveway when I looked to my left and saw a red Jeep Cherokee like John's parking next to the curb. I almost went down to my knees. My heart stopped as my brother-in-law, Jeff, got out of the driver's seat. From a distance, I thought it was John- more because of the car than the man coming towards me. He had

106

a case of Miller High Life in his hand, the champagne of beers. It was not even noon yet. I walked in with him, trying to forget the angry words from the night before, as that was his grief. I was still hurting, but so was he.

Not long after his arrival, I received a call from the deputy sheriff who responded to the call on the accident. I wrote his name down on the clipboard and his case number, too, before I misplaced the whole thing. He asked me some of the same questions that the officer and the medical examiner had the night before. "Did your husband have any medical conditions that you were aware of? Was he diabetic? Did he smoke? Drink? Text while driving?" I answered his questions the best I could. Before he hung up, he told me to call him if I had any questions regarding the accident. He also offered a copy of the report and explained that the medical examiner would have more information when everything was finished.

By this time, I needed fresh air again. So, I stepped out of the apartment door onto the sidewalk. I was waiting for someone to come. I was waiting for one of my friends to show. I was waiting for someone who wasn't related to the Geving's to come in my door just for me. I don't know why I felt that was important. I knew that his family was mine too, as we were married. However, I felt alone in that apartment full of people. I felt the burden of the situation laid solely on my shoulders. It was truly up to me to make my life work now. I no longer had a sidekick. I no longer had a better half. I no longer had a partner in this crime we call life.

Then, there was Tara, coming up my walk. She hugged me and rubbed my back. I don't remember, but I think Jo was with her. "How are you doing?" she asked.

"I don't really know." I looked at her and hoped that she could see how I was in my eyes, as I was incapable of articulating anything. I was not capable of telling her about how overwhelmed I felt. "The cell phones and talking are grating on my nerves."

"Where is Brooke?"

"She's inside."

"I was thinking that I would take her home with us and get her out of here for a while."

"That would be good," I told her.

"Do you have anyone to stay with you?"

"Yeah, Cally is going to stay here tonight and tomorrow," I said. She had offered to spend the night with me and told me she would be there later this afternoon.

"Good." We went into the apartment and there were cell phones ringing and people engaged in several conversations. I wanted to turn around and walk back out. But, I forced myself to stand there in the middle of my living room. Someone had pulled the chairs from around the kitchen table and placed them in the space, forming a circle of seating. The family was going to be there that afternoon, so that I could tell them John's wishes. Brooke asked not to be part of the discussion. It was good that she was going to Tara's.

Tara stayed for a bit, and then asked me if I needed her to stay longer. "No, get Brooke out of here. My Mom and brother will be here soon. We are going to discuss the funeral."

"Have you asked everyone to put their cell phones on vibrate?"

"Repeatedly," I said.

"I can tell the phones are overwhelming you."

"Well," I hoped I was smiling, "that isn't the only thing."

"Yeah," she laughed, "I bet it isn't."

The rolling string of people coming in and leaving my apartment was continuous, as were the phone calls from family and friends. I had to call my friend in Texas and tell her about John. I didn't want to tell her about my surprise visit, but I figured I should. It was hard because I was having a hard time remembering certain things. Stacey was one person that eluded me. I don't remember if I left her a message to call me, or if I actually got her when I called. The following week was her 40th birthday and I was supposed to be there.

When I reflect back on this, I remembered that she was supposed to be there for my 40th birthday too, but her step-father had passed and she didn't come. It felt too coincidental that for her 40th, I could not be there for her either. The voices whispered, "There are no coincidences."

"I know."

I was outside again, breathing in the fresh air. I was noticing the blue of the sky and could not see any clouds. "Shouldn't there be clouds?" I thought.

"Toni?" I heard from next to me.

Embarrassed because I thought I had said that aloud and someone heard me talking to myself, I looked to see Brooke. She was leaving with Tara, her bag jammed full of clothes. "Are you going?" I asked.

"Yes," she said.

"I know you said you don't want to help plan, but is there anything you want in the service for your dad?"

"Somewhere Over the Rainbow," she said, "and, bagpipes. Dad always wanted bagpipes."

"Yep, I know."

She gave me a kiss and a hug and went down the sidewalk. She was taking her car. "Why are you taking your car? I don't really think you should be driving."

"Why?"

"Because, I think you are overtired and grieving, and I don't really want you to be driving."

"I'll call you when I get to Tara's."

"Just text me," I said, a bit annoyed.

Tara gave me a hug and told me that she would make sure she got there safe. "I will have her text you when we get there."

"Thank you."

"She'll be fine."

"She needs to be back here Sunday night."

"I will make sure she is."

Evidently, someone had informed people that we were going to have discussion about the funeral at around 2, as everyone who wasn't immediate family had cleared out. John's brother and sisters and mom and dad were there. I don't remember if there were any other people, but these were the ones that had to be there. In one of my many phone calls, I had spoken to the medical examiner and to the funeral director at Cullen's funeral home. I wanted to see John before he was cremated. The medical examiner advised against it, due to the massive head trauma. However, the funeral director, Robert, said that he would arrange for that to occur after our discussion on the funeral on Sunday afternoon. First, I had to speak to the family about what John wanted.

I explained to the family that we would be meeting with the funeral director the following day at Cullen's. "I told the funeral director that I needed to see John's body before cremation. None of you have to be there for that, but this will be after we have our discussion with Robert."

"I want to see him too," Ann spoke up.

I cringed a little, as I was fully prepared for whatever it was I was going to see. I did not think that she was. "Ann, you do realize that he had severe head injury and he may not look very good? I do not want you to experience any further trauma," I told her as gently as possible.

"I know that," she said.

"Any of you who need to see him for closure are welcome to be there. Johnny wanted to be cremated and have his ashes scattered at the cabin. The Catholic Church will allow us to have his ashes in the church, as long as they are all together. There will not be an internment. John did not want to have a mass, so there will not be communion. I have not heard from the church yet on a date, but will talk to the funeral director tomorrow to make arrangements."

There were a few comments about his wishes and when we would scatter ashes. I had no clue when I would be ready to scatter his ashes, or how that would happen. I only knew that the family would have to be there. "It will be sometime this summer. I cannot tell you when right now. I haven't thought that far ahead."

John's brother was pretty quiet through everything. He did not interject anything with me. For some reason, I sensed he was angry with me. Maybe it was just left over feelings from the night before, or just an overall lack of trust? Whichever it was, I felt this energy and accepted it. I did not have to understand exactly what it was to know that it was there. I, myself, had anger and confusion too. I still wondered why it was him and not me that died. Why was I still here after my head injury? What purpose did this serve?

My mother-in-law, Shari, had told me that when she and Jack were both gone, she wanted their ashes mixed together and buried at the cabin somewhere. Although, at the time, I thought that would be something I could do with John's ashes, I realized later that it was not feasible. I was only forty-two years old and I had promised John that I would not remain single and unmarried for the rest of my life. I could not expect my second husband to mix my ashes with my first spouse! Even though I expressed interest in that, I knew by the end of the year I would not be doing this.

Chapter 9

Someone Call the Priest

On Sunday, March 29, 2009, I entered Cullen's Funeral home with John's family and Bill, his brother from another mother. John's high school friends were like his family, so it seemed fitting that Bill would be there with us, as we planned his service. My intention was to include his friends in the service as brothers. I was not clear going into the funeral home as to what that meant. My friend, Cally, was with me when I went to the funeral home. She had spent the night with me.

The funeral director, Robert, was a dark-haired man with a calm demeanor. He had kind blue eyes and was willing to assist me in whatever way I needed. He explained that we would go over the service arrangements and when all of that was done, he would roll John's body out on a gurney for whomever wanted to see him. I was not interested in prolonging anything for anyone. I just wanted to make the arrangements and go about my Sunday. I still have to call into work for the next week. There was no way I was going to be functional.

"I spoke with Father Jim this morning," Robert started the meeting. "He has five funerals this week and is leaving for the Chrism Mass in Superior this afternoon. The earliest we could have the service is Saturday morning. But, you need to call him today before he leaves."

"I tried calling the church yesterday," I said. "I left a message in the parish office for someone to get back to me."

"Well, try calling again, or go over there," he said.

The last thing I wanted to do was to go over and talk to a priest that I didn't know. John and I did not belong to the church in town. Jill did belong and she said that she spoke with someone in the parish office and they were aware of our wishes to have a service there.

"Then, someone should contact you," he said.

We went through what we wanted for John's service, explaining we did not want a mass and that we wanted to have his memorial before the service at the church. I told him that we would have picture boards and some other things representing John. He asked for John's social security number for the death certificate. I recited the number I had memorized. We created an obituary that represented the whole family and his friends. We toured the upstairs and looked at urns and caskets, which we knew we did not need. I purchased some lockets that held ashes for me and Brooke. As we were looking at urns, I explained that I would just put him in his tackle box, as that is what he wanted. Robert started talking about some of the ways people utilized ashes. "Some people load shotgun shells with them."

"I think you should shoot him out of a cannon," Bill suggested. "John would love that!"

The idea of shooting him out of a cannon like a circus clown made me smile. The idea took root in my head and I started wondering where the hell I could get a cannon. Could I get a cannon? I think the idea made his brother laugh. His dad was stoic as usual. But, I knew that John would appreciate the send-off. He would think it a grand idea. He was able to laugh at himself and not take life seriously. He was a clown.

As we completed the arrangements, Robert pulled me aside and told me that he needed a minute to get the body ready. "Did you want the clothes he came in with?" he asked me.

"No. I know that I could not handle that," I told him.

"I will give you his wedding ring and the other personal possessions that were in his pockets."

"That will be fine."

So, I explained to everyone there that he was going to go get John's body. "If you do not want to see him, you are free to go now." His father had already told me he did not want to see him and remember him that way. I appreciated that and told him he did not have to wait here.

116

"Toni," Bill said, concern in his voice, "are you sure about this?"

"I know that he had severe trauma," I explained, "but I have to see him for my own closure. I know that he may not look like himself, and I am prepared for that." Cally said that she did not want to see him and I was fine with that, too.

Robert wheeled him out and uncovered his face. His t-shirt was on him, covering up the autopsy incisions. His wedding band and the change in his pockets was in a red velvet pouch that had the name of the funeral home on it. Robert gave it to me and I handed it to Cally to put in my purse. "Take all the time you need," Robert told me. "He has some make-up on to cover some of the bruising and keep the skin moistened for viewing."

I approached the gurney with some hesitation. One of the things that I remember most about my father's wake was the smell. My mother had told me to kiss my father good-bye, as it would be the last time I saw him for a long time. At the age of six, the kiss to my father's cheek left a lasting impression. The smell, the feel of the cold flesh, and the stillness of death stuck in my mind for thirty-five years. Just upon entering the funeral home, I could smell that distinct smell of chemical preservative. On approach, I could tell this memory was building upon itself.

As I touched his arm and felt the cold, I realized that there was no spirit there. The soul had left the body. This cold, used body of my husband was vacant. Somehow, knowing that his soul was gone helped me here. The head was swollen and his lips appeared to be stitched closed. I touched his hair gently, knowing the receding hairline and ears. I saw his right arm had a laceration above the wrist. I touched his ears and his hand, just needing to feel his death a moment. My mind had pictured much worse than what greeted me here. His mother, sisters and brother also approached. I remember a couple tears dropping down off my chin onto my hand that held his. I wanted to honor his life by being strong enough to let him go.

"That's not him!" Ann said from the other side of the gurney.

"Yes, it is," I assured her. "I'd know those ears and chin anywhere."

Later, I found out that both his upper and lower jaw had been broken in the accident, which made his chin look even weaker than usual. The dimple in his chin was still there, but the swelling throughout his head made him look like someone else. I didn't want Ann to have any illusions about her son's passing. Though, I did not entirely agree with her decision to view his body, I knew that she needed closure, too. I was surprised that the four of them all came forward to see. Bill came forward, too. I don't know if he came forward to support me, in case I fell apart, or what. Ann had her other children. I had Cally and Bill. John was not there.

I looked at Jeff. He had tears in his eyes, but did not allow them to fall. His sisters were using tissues, as was his mom. I was not even conscious of the tears on my cheeks until they fell on my hand. I grabbed a tissue from the box on one of the tables. I wondered to myself how many boxes of tissues a funeral home goes through in a month, as I watched Jill empty a box.

When I was ready, I bent over and kissed John's cheek. Then, whispering in his cold ear, I told him I loved him and that I would do my best to live without him. In my head, I asked him to go in peace and help me understand why this was happening. I turned from the gurney and let his family say their last good-byes alone.

"Wow," Bill said from the meeting area, "he didn't look as bad as I thought. I was expecting worse."

"Me too," I concurred.

Jack overheard us and said, "I was expecting him to be worse too. But, from what I can see from back here, they did a pretty good job of preparing him. I just don't want that to be the last memory of my son."

"Jack, you need to remember him in blaze orange bagging that 9 point buck with you at the cabin." I don't remember if I actually said it aloud, but I remember thinking it. John had shot his buck two years earlier. Then, he caught a huge muskie with Bill and me on Bone Lake the summer before his death. Those were the memories I wanted to carry with me. Those were the memories I also wanted him to carry.

After leaving the funeral home, I remember going home and calling the parish office. As I had done the day before, I left another message. What I didn't know is that my mother-in-law was also leaving a message. One would think that someone from the church would call and talk to me about the funeral arrangements? I was getting really angry about it. I realized that two weeks before Easter was the most inopportune time for someone to die and have a funeral in a Christian faith organization, but what was happening? There were four funerals ahead of John's. I assumed that someone knew how to call back on funeral arrangements. If the priest wasn't going to call, someone else should!

Cally stayed with me while I stewed about the priest calling me. She was waiting for Brooke to come home and then, she was going to go home and go to her overnight position. She just listened. Then, she decided to clean my refrigerator. I watched her throw out jars and containers of food that we had not eaten. She wiped out the drawers, shelves and door. She made room for the food that everyone else brought. I watched her make short work of clearing it out. When she stopped, she asked, "I hope you don't mind and are not offended. This is how I could help right now."

"No, not offended. Thank you."

"What are you thinking?" she asked me. I think she noticed the tears in my eyes.

"I'm wondering why I am the one having to do this. Why was it him and not me?" I was thinking of Brooke coming home and wondering how I was going to help her, or if I could. She needed her father. She needed the parent that made her feel safe! He was her anchor and understood her. Why would God leave me to figure this out?

"Did you ever think," Cally said, "that God chose him because you are the strongest one? You are my angel on earth. I think you need to be here for others. Your head injury was your second chance."

"Huh?"

"John's here," she said. "He is kneeling in front of you telling you he is sorry and that he loves you. Brooke will be okay."

I could almost feel his hands on my knees. But, I couldn't see anything. Even the lights that were buzzing around the room earlier were, now, standing still. The whispers were silent for a moment. "I feel like I am going crazy!" I whispered. I told Cally what had been going on since my head injury.

"What do you think that is?" she asked.

"I don't know. I've actually seen angels with wings. I hear voices clear as day. What am I supposed to do with this? John even teased me about it."

"I've told you before that I think you are a transmedium. I think you are just finding it."

"I don't even feel like myself. I think every lobe of my brain was impacted by that blow to the head." I said. "I can't even cry like a normal person. It's like I knew he was going!"

"Maybe you did?" she said. "I believe we get information that our conscious mind is not ready to handle, so our unconscious mind stores it until we are."

"Well, that fucking sucks!" I laughed a little when I said it.

She laughed too. "That is kind of what started happening to me when I started massaging. I would see things leaving my client's body and get freaked out. You should talk to June or Chris. They helped me work through that."

"Maybe I will."

"I think John made the choice to go?" she said it like a question.

"What?"

"I think he left because he couldn't support who you were becoming."

"What?" I asked again.

"I don't know. It just came in the head and out the mouth," she laughed. "Do you ever have that happen?"

"Yes," I admitted. "It's like putting your foot in your mouth. You can't take it back once it is out there."

"Exactly!"

The two of us started talking about this information that seems to come from nowhere. A whisper in the ear, a dream, or just words tumbling out of the mouth, were all things that had happened to both of us. It freaked us out when our clients would look at us and wonder how we knew what we knew. They would ask and we couldn't tell them. Was this what a psychic gets? I really hated that word-psychic. "I'm not psychic!" I refused the idea.

Cally laughed. "Um, how about we call it intuitive?"

I didn't mind that word as much. The information came intuitively. Just like touch in a massage, I knew what amount of pressure to apply. I needed to be grounded and set my intention for the highest good of the client. Then, I would receive the gift of knowing. Our conversation tripped around the topic of psychic ability and fell into experiences we had. The lights in the room started moving again and the whispers confirmed some of the things we were saying. I felt the shifting inside of me. I was still grieving, but I was also awakening. How did that start? Was it just the suggestion? Was it just that grief got me out of my own way? I no longer was concentrating on how crazy I was feeling. I was looking at the task in front of me and wondering how I was going to deal with it.

When Brooke came home later that day, Cally was still there. I still had not heard from the church and was alternately ranting about the insensitivity of the priest and about changing to the Methodist church. I felt ignored. At the time, I realized that John and I did not belong to the parish. However, he did grow up in it and his daughter was baptized there. It just seemed like someone should have called by now. Brooke asked when the funeral was and I informed her that it would probably be Saturday, April 4th.

"I don't want to go to school this week," she said.

"Well, I understand that," I said. "But, this is your senior year and you really should not miss a lot of class."

"I just can't go."

As I had already called into work for the week, I understood what she was saying. How could I make her go to school when I could not even think about going into work? I decided to call the school in the morning and explain what was happening. "You will have to go back next week and you cannot miss anything more through the end of the year!"

"Next week is the Students Against Drunk Driving demonstration.   I   cannot   go   to   that   either."

"What is that?"

"You   know,   where   they   do   all   the   accident reenactment stuff? I don't want to see that!"

"What day is that?" I asked with a sigh. I knew she would not be able to handle it, as she just wasn't handling anything at the moment.

"Wednesday or Thursday."

"I can't believe they are doing that the week before Easter!" I complained.

"It might be the week after," Brooke said, with a sad look.

"Well, you find out when it is and we will deal with it."

Cally chatted with her a bit, while I tried to decide if there was anything I wanted to eat, other than the chocolate and peanut butter brownies that I had not finished. Cally and Tara agreed with me. They were not something that any of us really wanted to share. Thank God Brooke hated peanut butter!

I had spoken to Brooke's mother on the phone a couple times. She was drinking quite heavily and was not very helpful with making decisions for Brooke. So, I tried to make the best ones possible. As Brooke and Cally were talking, I thought I should ask, "Brooke? Have you talked to your mom?"

"Yes," she sighed.

"Why are you sighing?" I almost laughed.

"She tried to tell me that I needed to come home now and live with her."

"Oh? She did?"

"I told her that you need me now and my home is with you."

There was a place in the back of my mind where I felt that I was alone. I felt like I was making all these decisions, not knowing if they were the right ones, but trusting my gut. The decisions that I had made for Brooke's sake were the hardest ones, as she did not always like them and I had no legal responsibility for Brooke now. That belonged solely to Theresa, her mom. With this statement from her, I almost started to cry. She had unknowingly given me her trust and told me that she does feel safe with me. I looked at Cally with what I felt was an incredulous look. "Really?" I questioned.

"Yes," Brooke looked up at me. "I told her that my home has not been with her for two years. It has been with you and Dad. You need me."

Walking to Brooke, I gave her a big hug and thanked her. As her step-parent, I knew that she didn't always think I had the right to say anything. However, I know she knew I

126

had her best interest in mind in my decisions. John and I had many discussions with her about her decisions. We had many discussions with each other about her decisions. He understood her far better than I did, but he also knew I loved her. I could not help the tears that rolled down my cheeks as I held her. I was thanking God for that moment.

"See?" Cally said, when Brooke went into her room, "she does love you."

"Well, I knew that!"

Cally left for home early, as she was an overnight aide for a disabled adult home. She slept there for the night, and in the morning, got people ready for the day before she went to her full-time job. She had to go home before she went to work. She packed up her bag and told me that she would come back to spend the night on Thursday, if I needed her to do so. I explained that we would figure it out.

Chapter 10

Winning Bets

Monday morning was bright and sunny. I still hadn't slept more than a couple hours, nor had I eaten more than a sandwich... and the peanut butter brownies I should have hidden from everyone else. In addition, Nova was still pissed off that John wasn't there and showed his anger by pissing on my bed after I vacated my spot. For some reason, he was blaming me for the loss of his male companion. Yet, this finicky cat had no problem waking me up when he wanted food, and sitting on my lap for affection when I was on the couch. He slept on John's side of the bed most of the day and took up residence between my legs at night. It was quite amazing to see this cat grieving the loss of his male companion.

Still, I had not heard from anyone at the church. The priest was up in Superior and the parish office didn't seem to give a damn. However, I did get a call from the funeral director, Robert, asking me if I had contacted Father yet. I told him that I had not and that I was ready to change venues. He said, "Let me call over and talk to the office. You do not want to change venues." Although I knew he was right, I was extremely irritated that I had not received a call back from the parish office.   In my mom's parish, there was a whole committee of funeral volunteers that put on luncheons after mass. The volunteers of the parish did not even have to do that, as Jeff had arranged a caterer friend of his.

About an hour after I had spoken with Robert the first time, he called me back to tell me that I would be getting a call from Deacon Mike regarding the funeral on the 4th of April. Since we were not having a mass, the deacon could do the memorial service for John. I told him I would wait, as patiently as I could, for the call from the deacon. Sometime after one that afternoon, Deacon Mike did call me and left a message for me to call him back, as I had turned off the ringer on the phone by then.

Looking back on that week, I don't recall the specific order of events. However, I know that John's friend, Tim, flew in from Las Vegas on Tuesday. At about the same time, his friend, Karl, came from North Carolina. Most people do not understand why high school and childhood friends would come to a funeral so far away. Yet, John wasn't just anyone. John was their brother. He wasn't just their friend. He was family to them. It was important that they were there, and it meant more to me that they were.

At some point, Bill came over and was telling me that he had gotten in touch with John's friend, Mike. Mike was a very important part of John's life and only God knew why John felt he was his best friend. Many conversations were had by John and I about the person John swore would show up to be the best man at our wedding and didn't. The stories about this man were huge and, although humorous, very disconcerting to someone who cared about John. To me, this man did not care about anyone but himself, and had proven that to me on more than one occasion. I had never met this star of John's youth, who I had sworn to punch in the face should ever I have the opportunity. Yet, Bill came in to tell me that Mike was coming to John's funeral.

"I will believe that when I see him," I said with a scoff.

"He's coming," Bill said. "He has to get off work and he will leave Wednesday."

"Whatever," I said. "April Fools!"

"He's coming."

"He's going back to Denver with a black eye!"

"What makes you say that?" Bill asked.

"Bill," I sighed, "Mike has not been there for the most important moments in Johnny's life. Why would he be here for the last? The man is not showing up!"

"I know you are bitter about him not showing up for your wedding. You need to forgive him for that. He will come."

"Forgive him?" I asked, incredulous. "I'm not holding my breath on Mike!"

Every day that week, I got an update on the weather in Denver and Mike's plan to leave from Bill, who clung to the idea with faith in his friend. He told all of the Geving's that Mike was coming. He told Tim, Karl, Jeff, Mark and I when we went out for drinks one night. That night, we placed bets and put the money in my Bible under Judges 15:16 regarding Samson killing thousands with the jawbone of an ass. Everyone agreed with me that Mike would not show his face at the funeral. Bill had unwavering faith in all of his friends and God. Yet, I was still figuring out how God played into any of this.

When he called later in the week and talked to me, saying he was very sorry to hear about John and that he was unable to make it to the funeral, I held my anger in check. Then, he spoke to Brooke and promised her that "Uncle Mike" would come see her in the summer, I got even more pissed off. I knew he just gave Brooke another false promise. It made me mad that people made promises that they did not keep. I knew that I had unintentionally made promises that I had not kept, although I fully intended to keep them when I made them. I knew Mike would not keep his promise to Brooke. Although I don't know for sure, I don't think he ever intended to visit her.

Wednesday was April Fools' Day and our mild weather turned into slushy snow flurries. Ironically, that was the day that John received a $900 bill from the United Fire and Rescue in Baldwin for highway cleanup and extracting him from the vehicle. This was just one of the many things that made me angry in the days following John's accident. I wasn't even angry at him for dying. I just was angry at the stupidity of people. John's accident required that he be pried out of the car with the Jaws of Life that the fire department uses when metal in crumbled and bent into metal. Why would they send a bill to the man that they knew was dead? I almost resealed the envelope and returned it to the sender. Instead, I put it aside and stewed about that and about the priest that didn't have time to call me.

Another irritant I had was to call the school every day to let them know Brooke would not be attending class because of the death of her father. The first day I called, I received a call back from the secretary telling me that I would have to call every day. What kind of jackass made that rule? However, I was not her legal guardian, so I did it every day.

It was Wednesday when I received a call from my employer. The Human Resources person called to tell me that I only had three days of bereavement pay, but I could take the time off unpaid, or with any available vacation pay I had. As I was supposed to fly to Texas the next day and was taking vacation anyway, I told the Human Resources flunky that I was fine with taking it unpaid until I was ready to come back, which I believed would be the following Monday. I was angry, but not at her. She was doing her job. I was angry because I was thinking, "How does the average person get enough strength to go back to work a week after their spouse dies in a horrid accident? What would constitute more time for this company? Would they hold my job for me if I had to take more time?" Then, I realized that I was anything but average. Plus, I knew there was God somewhere in this, even if I couldn't see him yet. It didn't make me less angry, but it allowed me to tolerate stupidity. Truly, it was stupid to think a spouse could go back to work after three days!

At some point during my conversation with this "relay girl," I realized that she didn't expect me back the following Monday. I don't think anyone expected me back that day. All she was telling me was that they would not pay me for not doing my job. Well, that wasn't any surprise to me. I knew that from my head injury. Nobody was going to feel sorry for me because I no longer had a spouse and couldn't add numbers in my head. I didn't want anyone to have pity for me. I wanted compassion and empathy, not pity.

When in the situation of dealing with the death of a loved one, most people dwell on their own experience of grief and cannot see that there are differences in how each affected individual deals with it. As an example, Brooke became hostile and angry with anyone who did not show her the level of empathy that she felt was appropriate. Jack did not show his grief by sharing tears, but he became even more stoic- if that was even possible. Ann concentrated on the fact that her son was gone and seemed to take on some guilt. In addition, she would start to grieve her husband, who had been gone seven years, and lump it all together with other situations of grief that she had not dealt with in previous years. In many ways, I saw people putting their grief and pain before mine.

As an observer, I was just overwhelmed by the lights and sounds that I had been seeing for months. Adding the lights and sounds of everyone's grief was enough to silence my own. I didn't want to see it. I didn't want to become a slobbering mess every time someone mentioned John. I wanted a quiet place to just be still. I wanted to have just one moment with John to say good-bye. I wanted my own time with him, not something I had to share with everyone else.
The Bible says that a man leaves his mother and clings to his wife. It made me angry that I felt like I needed to remind John's mother of this. Was it wrong that I wanted to shout at her, "He was not yours anymore!?"

Of course, I never shouted anything at her. I may have ranted in my apartment and talked to myself in the mirror, when I was alone. However, I would never have done that to anyone. I knew that everyone had their own grief and their own way of grieving. We all could share our experiences. However, not everyone would be willing to receive the knowledge at the time we wanted to share it. For some reason, I knew that I was not ready to grieve and that I just needed to be present for others who were ready. So, I did a lot of watching and listening that week. I was processing it all.

My sisters came over for lunch and shopping that week, too. We took Brooke out to shop for a dress for Prom, even though we did not know if she was going. Then, we went over to Jill's house and helped with putting pictures on boards for the memorial service. It was that day that my sister, Angie, nicknamed Jill's husband, Tom, "Pumpkin". We were going through pictures and came across a picture of Michael carving a pumpkin. Tom was standing in the background in his underwear. We all were laughing because of Angie's animated response to seeing him this way. Shortly after seeing this picture, Tom came home from work and appeared in the living room to see what we were doing. Angie smiled and said, "Hi Pumpkin!"

Laughter was one of the things that helped ease the pain of missing John. It was one of the things that made me think about him, too. We could get each other laughing just by laughing. We didn't even have to be laughing at anything in particular. It helped to remember that John easily laughed at himself and found humor in simple things. Looking at pictures of him, it was easy to remember the humor he had.

When my sisters brought Brooke and I home, we had many happy memories in our heads. The sun had burned through the slush-rain clouds and left the ground wet. Brooke wanted to go to Tara's for the rest of the week. I agreed half-heartedly, as I would be alone in the apartment for the first time. But, I had to get used to being alone again, so I let her go. Plus, I knew that I wasn't alone. I could see that I was never alone.

One day that week, my mom and Craig came and we went and had burgers at Champs, in New Richmond. John knew the owners and really liked the bar. It had closed because of a fire and was reopened. The burgers there were huge and it was one of my favorite places in town. John and I spent Christmas Eve in this bar until 3 AM the first year we were dating. He used to go in and talk about weight lifting with George. George knew that John had a taste for spicy and used to let John taste test his chili as he was putting it together. So, we had dinner there and I was hoping to tell George and Linda that John had died. However, they probably already knew by this time. I just wanted to be there and have a beer for John.

Throughout the week, I ran into people that knew John, or another one of the Gevings. People introduced themselves to me, whenever I was out. Months after his death, I would run into people that knew me through John. It was weird seeing the reactions of people when I told them John was dead.

The New Richmond News, which I lovingly refer to as the "town rag" came out on Wednesdays. The front page story was about John's accident. It explained that he had crossed the center line, side-swiped a car and had a front-end collision with another car. The Rag went on to say that he was the third fatality in St. Croix County this year and that the fourth and fifth happened the same night. I bought a couple papers on Thursday from the Kwik Trip up the street from our apartment. I don't know why I felt the need to buy more than one. It wasn't like I was scrapbooking John's death. I knew I would have plenty of information to read in the coming weeks and months. But, somehow, it seemed important to buy more than one paper. Though, I took the papers home and put them on my kitchen table, where they sat for months afterward.

On Friday, Bill asked me if I wanted to go for a walk. The weather was better and the snow was melting again. As Brooke had gone back to Tara's, I realized that I needed to get out for a bit and agreed to go for a walk with him. He told me to drive to this county park outside of New Richmond. It was the place where his brother had killed himself. I am not sure why he wanted to take me there, but I felt that John's death made him think about his brother's death, too. John and his brother, Ron, were the two closest friends to Bill.

We parked in the little lane that went into the park. It was blocked off by a fence. The gravel road was clear, so we got out and walked down to the river that ran through part of the park. There was a meadow of grass that was turning green with little snowbanks around the perimeter. As we walked over the little stream, I noticed animal prints in the mud. There were three sets of them, one larger and two sets of smaller prints. I didn't say anything to Bill, but knew that these were black bear paw prints in the mud. Cautiously, I looked around and talked a little louder than I had been talking.

Bill told me that he had done some duck and goose hunting in this park when he was younger. He had many stories of his youth that he and John had relayed while sitting on the couch in our living room watching sports events. This was his time to talk and I listened. At some point, I determined that I could outrun Bill if I had to, should the mother bear come back with her cubs and feel threatened. Although, I did not think it was that much of a threat, it was spring and hibernation was over.

As he finished his story of ducks and geese, I asked him, "Bill, did you notice the bear tracks over by the stream?"

"What?" he asked.

We had turned to walk back towards the car and I was almost back to the paw prints. I pointed to what I knew were bear prints. He went over and looked down at the tracks in the mud. "Those are bear prints!"

"Yes," I said, "I know."

"We better get out of here. I don't want to have to explain to the Gevings that you got mauled by a bear."

"I am pretty sure that I could outrun you," I laughed.

"Funny."

"Though, I don't want to explain a double funeral either."

We got back to the Jeep and drove home. I was a bit turned around by our trek to the park. I was pretty sure that I wouldn't be able to find the park again on my own. My sense of direction was a bit skewed since I hit my head. The only thing I was sure of was up and down, left and right. Though, I remembered later that the park was north and east of my apartment.

We went back to my place and sat to talk for a while. As we sat there, the weather turned to rain again. Eventually, Bill went home and I found something else to do. Although I don't remember everything, so many things stuck out in my mind. I found laughter that week in remembering Johnny and a little peace. However, I don't remember having many crying

139

jags. There were moments when tears leaked out of the corners of my eyes to trickle down my cheek. With the exception of the shower, I just did not cry. There were times when I wanted to yell and scream and swear at God, but I didn't do that either. I just accepted that there was a reason in this. I knew that God was working somewhere in this heartache. And, the lights and whispers around me encouraged that line of thinking.

Chapter 11

The Wife

Saturday, April 4, 2009 started early for me. John's funeral was scheduled for 12:00 PM with a visitation at the church beforehand. Again, Cally had spent the night Friday night and Brooke was supposed to be home before the service. Of course, she was late. The night before, I decided to wear black trousers with a dark purple top. But, I didn't like how it looked. I don't know why I agonized over what I was going to wear. It was a funeral, for goodness sake, not a party! Besides, I wanted people to remember John for the brilliant star he was. Nobody cared what I was wearing!

"Why don't you wear this blouse?" Cally asked, holding up a new blouse I had bought for my trip to Texas. It was a wrap blouse with a collar and it was red. Not that mousy, cross between pink and rose, but a bright, vibrant red color.

"I can't wear that!" I protested.

"Why not?" Cally scoffed mildly.

"It's red!"

"So?"

"Can I wear red to a funeral?"

"John would want you to look your best. You look great in red!"

I thought about that a moment. She was right. John wouldn't care if I wore jeans to his funeral. He would want me to be the woman of strength that he married. To me, there was no other color more powerful than the fire of red. All at once, I realized it was up to me to show everyone that I was still standing and this wasn't going to take me out. So, I put it on and tied the wrap fabric in a bow to the side and looked in the mirror. The lights around me seemed to nod in approval and the voices said, "Yes! That's perfect!"

"Wow! That is the person Cheetos fell in love with!" Cally said. "You look strong and beautiful!" She smiled and went to put on her make-up. I sat on the bed and applied mine with my hand mirror.

We chatted while we both worked on our faces. I knew Jeff and Karla were coming by the apartment before going to the church. We had time to fill. I don't remember what we were talking about when Cally suddenly squeaked, "Oh my God!"

"What?" I asked, concerned at the panic in her voice.

"Nova, get it!" She squealed.

"What is wrong?" I asked, coming around the corner into the bathroom. She was pointing at a black spider on the ground. The cat was just looking at it and Cally was standing on the wall of the bathtub. I started to laugh, remembering that she was afraid of spiders. When the spider moved, the cat pounced on it, playing with it rather than killing it.

"Get it Nova!" Cally urged.

"Are you kidding me? He will play with that thing for hours before he kills it." I grabbed a tissue and reached down to squish the spider and flushed it down the toilet.

"How can you do that?"

"I don't know. I used to just step on them with my bare feet until I lived in Texas. Some of the spiders there are poisonous."

"Eww!"

"My sister was afraid of them too. She used to call me from the basement," I laughed. Just then, Jeff and Karla showed up at the door. "Come in, it's open."

They came in the door and Karla was wearing a skirt. Jeff was wearing a shirt and tie. They looked nice. Cally and I were not done with our spider conversation and continued as if not interrupted. "Karla's afraid of worms," Jeff said.

"Really?" Cally asked.

"Yes. They are just gross," Karla confessed.

We all started talking about things we didn't like. My big fear of snakes was more understandable to me than fearing a spider, or a worm. Jeff was saying something about those centipede things that were in the basement. Then, he looked down at Karla's foot and said, "Karla, there is a worm on the floor by your foot."

Karla screamed and jumped when she looked down. The 'worm' Jeff saw was actually a black scuff in the linoleum floor of my kitchen. The tenants before John and I had splattered hot grease all over the floor, causing the floor to melt and scorch in places. Upon realizing that the "worm" was nothing but a blackened indent in the floor, Karla pushed Jeff hard with her hand. He laughed and shook his head.

"You jerk!" she said. Then, she laughed with the rest of us.

As we stood there in my kitchen laughing, I realized that my stomach had settled a little bit. I realized that I wasn't so scared to go to the church. For some reason, I had knots of tension in my stomach that morning. I don't know why I thought the memorial service for John would mean that I had to say good-bye for good. It was quite ridiculous to even think that I would not think of him, remember little things about him, or grieve him after that day. However, the accumulation of the activities of the week was a vehicle to get us to this day. I had no clue what was going to happen. I had no idea how I would feel. Why did I feel this tension? Why did I want to throw up? Why did I have to go through the death of my spouse?

The voices were not talking. Cally seemed to know there were Spirits in the room, as we both had seen my deceased father in the massage room and my guardian angel, Timothy. I felt them there, but could only see lights and hear whispers. Then, there was this feeling that John was there, but couldn't talk to me. The preliminary autopsy had come that week and said that both his upper and lower jaw were broken by the airbag. I had read that preliminary report and understood that he had atherosclerosis with 'visible narrowing of the LAD'. My school anatomy paid off there, as it gave understanding to the information I was receiving from the voices. What the voices did tell me was that John had a stroke while driving that may have been caused by a clot dislodging and going to his brain. The trauma to his head would hide the actual cause of his accident. Although I trusted all the information that I received from Spirit, I could not share the information with everyone without those people looking at me like I had lost all touch with reality. The whole situation of the death of my spouse felt unreal- like an awful dream.

Jeff and Karla drove to the church in their car and I went separately with Cally, as Brooke was not going to make it home to go with us. I knew she would be late, even though I asked her to come home the night before. She came with Tara and Jo. I brought John's empty tackle box into church and gave it to Robert to put his ashes inside. Looking around in the sacristy, I saw picture boards covered in many pictures of John and his family. There were a few of our wedding and some of him with Brooke as a baby. Jill really worked hard to put together wonderful pictures.

On a table amidst the pictures, there was also a trombone. Tim brought it to honor John's love of music and time playing the trombone in marching band together. In addition to the loan of his instrument, Tim wrote a nice piece in honor of John that was on the back of his memorial card that John's cousin put together. There was also a picture of John and Brooke on the front of the memorial card. Tim was able to put together the words that were failing me in that moment.

Deacon Mike came up to me and asked me if there was anyone who was going to say a eulogy. I hadn't thought that far ahead and I didn't want anyone to feel like they had to do this. I wanted his brothers to bring him up to the altar and place him there. So, I asked Jeff, Karl, Tim, Mark, Bill and Tammy, Johnny's friend's wife, to honor him this way. Tony was in Texas getting ready to deploy to Iraq with Tara's husband. His wife, Tammy, was there in his place. She didn't have to come, but I was grateful she did.

In the back of the church, there was a line of people by the pews. I had no place of honor and felt like I just took up a spot by the pews. As the 400 plus people started coming in and going through the pictures, I could hear people say, "Is that the wife?" After hearing it more than a handful of times, I was getting a bit frustrated. I'm the one who knew all of John's secrets, his wishes, and his greatest advocate and people were calling me "the wife" like I was the problem in the room?

It amazed me who showed up at a funeral. There were people from work that came in and paid their respects. They hugged me and told me they were glad that I wore red. In addition, one of John's old bosses and several friends from the company where he'd been laid off in February were there. There were clients of mine, relatives and family friends there. I even had friends that I had just reconnected with come from the other side of the Twin Cities and northern Minnesota. My school buddies and some of John's were there. At one point, I realized I had to go to the bathroom before the service started and had no way of getting there.

So, there was no eulogy. Deacon Mike seemed to capture the information on John from listening to people talk at the visitation and used it in the service. We even had a bag piper playing "Amazing Grace" at the beginning of the service. It was exactly what John said he wanted. Bagpipes, lots of pictures of him having fun, and friends and family were what he wanted. In his life, he rarely liked being alone. He wanted his death to be a party, too.

I wanted John's family to be able to sit in the reserved seats with Brooke and me. I wanted my mom there too. But, the Catholic Church had this monstrosity of an organ in the middle and the reserved seating was reduced to small pews. Then, Brooke had to have Jo sitting next to her in the front. Rather than telling her Jo could not sit up there, I crammed 5 people into the front pew.

I did what I could to accommodate everyone else's feelings. I can remember sitting in that pew thinking, "I wish I would have told the deacon that I would say something. I'm calm. John deserves a few words." But, I just let it go. If someone had something to say, they would voice their words later to the people that mattered to them.

For some reason, I wondered if people understood that I was not ready to cry. I felt a few tears slide down my face, but I wasn't about to start sobbing at his funeral. Or, were people wondering why I wasn't crying? Were they wondering why I was wearing red to a funeral? Were they going to talk about me later? "Who cares?" I heard in my ear. I think I kind of jumped a bit. Then, I smiled. It was getting harder to sit still in the pew. I don't know if it was Brooke crying next to me, or my mother-in-law sniffing on the other side of my mother, but I realized, at this point, John would be pulling some episode of "Seinfeld" into his head and laughing at Kramer. He did this when I made him go to church. He would get the giggles, and holding it in, would make him cry. I almost started to laugh at the memory of him laughing through Easter Sunday mass at my mother's church.

His green and gray tackle box sat up on a table by the sanctuary. All of his body reduced to ashes that would fill a crematorium box that was six inches wide, two inches deep and 11 inches high. The plastic bag with his ashes was in the tackle box and the ugly brown box from the crematorium was somewhere in the back, among the things I would take with me when I went.

Before I knew it, the service was over and we were headed downstairs for the luncheon Jeff's friends had prepared. Pulled pork, baked beans, Au Gratin potatoes, coleslaw, and a bunch of deserts were laid out for the guests in the social hall in the basement of the church. Karla had called me earlier that week when she and Jeff were planning the luncheon. "Toni, what did John like to eat?"

The pregnant pause before my answer suddenly erupted with laughter on both sides of the phone. "Um, what didn't he like to eat?" I laughed.

So, everything that was served would have been approved by John. It was like a party, except there was no beer. And, the only reason why there was no beer was because we were in a church. The family ate. My brother and his wife and daughters had come from Ohio and were planning on leaving after the funeral for their annual Florida vacation. They ate and left for an even longer drive. My mom was going home with one of my other siblings. John's cousins and siblings were meeting for drinks that night and then breakfast the following morning. Tim, Mark, and Karl were going to hang around for a bit. I was suddenly tired, and overwhelmed, and just wanted to go home. In a room full of several hundred family members and friends, I realized that the only one that I wanted to turn to was in a tackle box upstairs. So, with a smile and some determination, I started asking people to help pick up plants, flowers and memorabilia and load it in cars.

Cally had left after the funeral with her mother to go to Walmart. She was going to meet me back at the apartment. Brooke was already there, when I arrived. She was already whining about going back to Tara's and school on Monday. I explained to her that I was going back to work, so she would have to go back to school. I tried to be patient when she acted like nobody had it worse than her. I tried to understand that her grief was not allowing her to see that other people had suffered through losing their father at a young age. I was only 6 when I lost mine. I wanted to tell her how hard this was for me, but she would not be able to see that until she was older. She would not be able to see how much it hurt that I was viewed as "the wife."

One of the most profound things that I noticed during that week after John's death was that while everyone was experiencing their own grief, their grief was more important to them than that of others. For example, I understand that no parent should ever have to go through the death of a child. But, it does happen. The grief of a parent is not more weighted, or worse than the grief of a spouse. It is just different. I could not relate to the death of a child, as the children I lost were not born. But, I could relate to the death of a father. I could relate to the death of a spouse. And, I found myself angry with a couple of my in-laws, as they did not understand that John had made his life with me and he was my other half. Yet, his mother lamented to Brooke and I about the loss of her son, as if it was greater than our experience.

Several weeks later, I was explaining to Bill this feeling of being pushed into a corner, when he said, "The Bible says that a man shall leave his mother to become one with his wife. So, I understand why you feel a bit slighted. But, you need to understand that she is grieving too."

"You don't think I know that?" I asked, incredulously. "I haven't said anything to her, or anyone, about the things they have said since he died that is in contradiction to the treatment they gave him while he was alive."

"What do you mean?"

"Jeff told me that Ann was reprimanding John on his drug use at the bar before he left that day. And, John just took it. He just had another beer."

"What?"

"She acted like he hadn't overcome that. Why do they all throw his past transgressions in his face?"

"John has never been one to fight back," Bill stated.

"Yes, I know. Do you know that Tom told me one time that John is a "baby" because he wants everyone to fix his problems?"

"What?"

"Yeah, he looked me right in the eye and said that. I asked John what he meant and John said, 'Well, some people forget about the help that others gave them and look down on others because they ask for help.'"

Bill started to laugh and agreed that John knew what he was saying. "I think John didn't care what others thought about him because he knew their flaws too."

"John was so non-confrontational! He would not say shit if he had a mouth full of it!"

"He gets that from his dad."

"Yep."

"But, you know, I have never heard one negative comment come out of John's mouth about Theresa and I have never heard Jack say one bad thing about Ann. Yet, John and Jack have both had their names dragged through the mud by both of those women. Is it a woman thing?"

"You don't do that," he remarked.

"Not intentionally. I guess I am angry about how everyone forgets the good things John did. He never stuck up for himself. If I had not encouraged him, he would never have gone back to school and graduated."

"True." Bill said. "Toni, if you had died instead of Johnny, I think that I would have still lost my best friend. John would not be the person he had become without you."

"Huh?"

"Without you, that John would disappear and nobody would be able to find him."

"Why do you say that?"

"You changed him. You made him want to survive and be someone better. He knew how lucky he was to have you. He told me so."

"Well, I think we changed each other, because in another time, I would have come out swinging and left no nose unbloodied." I laughed as I said it.

"What are you saying?"

"I'm saying there are times when I want to punch them all in the mouth for the shit they say. Theresa, Ann, Jeff and maybe his sisters on occasion," I explained, "need a punch in the mouth. But, I would not do that now. They all have said things about me and John behind our backs. Don't get me wrong, I know they loved John. But, I don't know how many times they would not allow the past be in the past."

"I hear you."

"I realize this anger towards them is part of my grief," I explained. "However, some of it is resentment that I carried from before. Some of it I said to John and he told me to just let go of it and not care what anyone says about him or me. He was better at letting go of those things."

Chapter 12

Getting Angry

June 5, 2009

United Fire Rescue District

To Whom It May Concern:

I am writing because I received the enclosed invoice dated 5/10/09 and addressed to my deceased spouse, John W. Geving. My husband died in the accident for which you are billing extrication and overtime hours.

Although I do understand your need to bill for services rendered, I question why you send an invoice to a dead man? One would think your organization would have known that he would be unable to pay this bill, as it was your organization that extricated his lifeless body from the vehicle. Further, I would guess that your organization would have communication with the responding sheriff and would have the ability to find out an appropriate avenue to take in collecting for your fees.

As you can see, this letter is not a refusal to pay, as I have enclosed a check for the full balance of the invoice. However, I would like to suggest that you review your billing practices for the future. It is still a crime for someone to open the mail of another person, unless directed by that person to do so. As my husband is dead, he could not direct me to open his mail, which put me in an unethical and legal situation. Please consider this going forward, as losing my husband was traumatic and very stressful.

Respectfully,
Toni Geving

Yes, I was angry when I wrote it, but it felt so good to send it. Maybe I was stupid to pay it, but I was dealing with lots of stupid things. For example, I paid a $125 garbage bill from the sanitation company. After paying the bill, I went through everything and realized they had charged me twice. Through their sloppy accounting, they hadn't applied my money correctly; I am not so sure that they didn't have two accounts. I was so frustrated with all of these bills. I never cared enough to look into it further.

At about the same time I wrote this letter, I wrote one to the Archbishop of the Catholic Church in Superior. It was equally as sarcastic and bitchy as my letter to the Fire Department. Much to my chagrin, I never received any response to either letter. It was a couple years before I could go back into Immaculate Conception in New Richmond. Ironically, the reading and homily of that mass I attended were on forgiveness. I knew I was supposed to be there that day. When I wrote these letters, I was a long way from forgiveness. I was just coming into the anger of grieving.

Grief came in waves for me. I was not always sad. I was not always angry. Yet, the voices that I heard were continuous, keeping me up at night. I was seeing lights move with shadow and taking different forms. However, I was not sure if the voices and images were the after-effects of my head injury, or something to do with grief. I started to wonder if it was both. Could I have one without the other? Could I have the grief and cope without the whispered voices giving me direction? Would I be coping as well as I was if I had not knocked myself senseless on that sidewalk in January? What purpose did all this serve?

There were two major events that happened after John's death. The first was Brooke's graduation from high school and all the drama that included. The second was her eighteenth birthday in June. She continued to live with me and had issues going to school. At one point, she didn't even want to graduate. She had four weeks left and she told me she wanted to drop out. Unfortunately, there were the usual bitchy girls harassing and bullying her. I would go into school and talk with her guidance counselor, only to be told I had no legal authority whatsoever. Somehow, I convinced her to persevere.

One of the things I did was to get Brooke into counseling. She had six sessions with the counselor, who was just starting to see the anger this girl had inside. Then, she turned eighteen and knew everything. It is amazing how we feel that our age dictates our ability to make appropriate decisions for ourselves. So, while I continued going to counseling every 4 weeks, Brooke said she wasn't going. This was further enforced by her biological mother's opinion that counseling did nothing for anyone. Theresa had vocalized this to Brooke and me on several occasions. She vocalized a lot of things in those months- usually while highly intoxicated on alcohol. Theresa talked to me more about how angry she was with John. She showed more anger than I ever voiced to anyone. In fact, I don't think I was ever angry with John. I found other things to be angry about.

All of a sudden, Brooke did not feel like she had to call me and tell me she was going to be late. I had bought a car, using my credit, for her to have, provided she made payments. That lasted about 2 months. She didn't want to follow any of my rules. She didn't want to work. She didn't want to be here at all. Yet, she would not talk to me, or a counselor, about this and work through her stuff. She became more angry and resentful of me, often using her father as a weapon to hurt me. On one day before school ended, she told me that she had problems with me before her father married me. Then, she told me that her father would not have married me if she had not given him permission. Both times she was lashing out and I felt the sting. Then, I realized that John would never have allowed her to dictate his happiness in that way.

During one particularly heated argument, Brooke told me that she wished I was the one who had died in that accident. Then, she stomped out the door and left. I remember thinking, "Yeah, me too!" To which, the voices became louder and told me to disband that way of thinking. They were letting me know that, somehow, John's death would be for nothing if I did not continue pushing through this. It was not like I would ever do anything to hurt myself. Yet, there were times when I just felt like giving up. I did not want anyone to know how vulnerable I really was. Cally was the only one who had seen me cry hard, and that was on the massage table when John appeared to her there.

On Brooke's eighteenth birthday, I received a call from the St. Croix County impound lot asking me if I wanted to have the car moved. I had seen pictures of John's Jeep Cherokee. I still have them on my computer. I was at work and was trying to figure out what to do. When I asked what my options were, I was told that I could have it towed myself, or the county would dispose of it. Although part of me wanted to go through that vehicle, I just did not think it was worth the emotional trauma that action would cause. I told them that I only needed the keys on his key ring that were not returned in the evidence bags and that they could dispose of the vehicle. There was no cost to me for them to do this.

The St. Croix County Medical examiner was fabulous! He delivered copies of the coroner's report to Jack personally, not charging us for that. We received a copy of the accident report with all the witness statements, too. He never came to me. At times, I felt really bad that Jack had to deal with that for me. I don't know why I leaned on him so heavily. I wonder if it had something to do with the fact that John was so much like his father that it was a comfort. It was hard not to lean on him- The Stoic One. Though he didn't share his feelings with just anyone, I knew he felt John's loss greatly. I knew that his taking the role of information gatherer was a gift he was giving me. I asked him if he would mind receiving that information and he said he would do it.

Bill would come over and watch television with me. We'd go out to dinner, or to the casino to "take their money." I went because it got me out of the apartment. For me, he was like a brother that knew John as well as I did. He and I had both lost our best friend. It made sense that we would share our lonely moments so that we weren't so lonely. But, that was short-lived because Bill took an over-the-road trucking job with Swift and drove through the holidays. He'd call me from the road and ask for directions and information on where he could go to get things to eat. He always had stories. I could hear Johnny laughing and see him shaking his head. "Only Bill," he would say of his friend's uncanny ability to fall into the worst-case scenario every time he was presented with one.

The summer went by slowly. I had no real ambition to do any of the things that John and I did together. Fishing, camping, going to the cabin and hiking through the woods were things that John and I did. We'd go up to the cabin and fish off the docks and dams. I was not ready to experience the quietness of a lake without John. I wasn't going to go to my father-in-law's cabin by myself, as I knew John was there in spirit. I knew that is where he would go. Yet, I could feel him. Some days, I could smell his Old Spice underarm deodorant.

Towards the end of August, I did finally go to the cabin with family and we scattered some of John's ashes in a small family gathering. My mom and one of my brothers were there. Jill, Tom and the kids, Jack and Shari, Ann and Brooke were there to scatter ashes. Everyone had the opportunity to say something. I could feel John there. His presence was palpable. Brooke scattered ashes in the outhouse, stating that her Dad liked to shit and would appreciate being close to a toilet. When we left, I felt bad that more people could not be there.

Then, towards the end of the month and my anniversary, Cally and I went back up to the cabin. We drank a case of beer while sitting on the deck, talking most of the night. We laughed a lot. Then, the next day, we put some of John's ashes into a couple potatoes, stuck them into a potato launcher I had made, and shot him into the trees off the deck. Then, we went fishing off the dam.

It was a beautiful day for fishing. Cally had just put new line on her rod and we were fishing off the boat launch when her line started tangling up. As she untangled 20 yards of fishing line, I just cast off into the water, laughing at her. The game warden came up to the dock in a boat, asking to see our licenses while laughing at Cally's mess of fishing line. After an hour of detangling, she was finally ready to do some fishing and we moved down below the dam.

I was sitting on some rocks casting into the lake below and felt this tingling beside me. Cally was standing knee deep in water and she was looking up at me. "Oh my God!" she whispered, as I looked at the brilliant white light next to me. There, sitting next to me on the rocks, was John in a white t-shirt, blue jeans and work boots. He was beautiful and bright and so perfect that it hurt to look at him. I could see him smiling at me, and felt his love burning into my chest and going straight to my heart. "Do you see?" Cally whispered below me.

"Yes!" I whispered, as tears started to fall down my cheeks. He smiled and kissed my cheek, leaving a tingly feeling there. He didn't say anything. He just picked up his ethereal pole and started casting into the water before becoming part of the sunlight. Then, he was gone.

Cally came out of the water to sit next to me and I could see she was crying too. "Oh my God!" she breathed. "He was beautiful! You saw him, right?"

"Yes. I felt him kiss me."

"How do you explain that to anyone?" she said in almost a whisper. "I've never seen anything like it Toni!"

"I know. It was like he had the light of God behind him."

"Yes. He felt good."

"I know," I said. "Did he say anything?"

"No. But, he gave us a gift by letting us see him."

"Cally, I think I am seeing more than just him. I cannot put my finger on it, but it feels like his visit here is huge."

"Duh! Of course it is huge! I don't know anyone else who gets visited by angels."

"I think it happens a lot. We just don't know it."

"Probably."

We fished for a couple hours before we realized we were hungry. Once we packed up our gear and got back in the car, we decided we were going to stop for a Bloody Mary and something to eat. "I don't like Bloody Marys, but I know a place that makes them really well, just down the road from here."

"I'm so hungry I could eat my arm," Cally claimed. So, we stopped for Bloody Marys and a burger at The Lookout. They have a Bloody Mary that is a snack, with a shrimp prawn, hard-boiled egg, beef stick, stuffed olive and a beer chaser. Or, you can get it without the snack. This is the option I chose, as I wanted a burger, too. Cally decided that it was the best Bloody Mary she had ever had and I agreed.

When we got back to the cabin, we talked about our experience at the dam and seeing John. We compared notes. We both agreed that seeing John was one of the most powerful and beautiful things either of us had witnessed. It surpassed seeing my eagle- like angel, Timothy, landing on the massage table so that I could talk to my dad. Was it because I could physically see him and feel him in front of me, or because Cally saw the same thing? I don't know. However, that sighting of John burned away the image of his corpse on the gurney in the funeral home. I realized that Ann was right. That was not John. His soul had left already. That was just the shell of his body. Without the soul, it really wasn't John.

Chapter 13

Floating Lights

After seeing the Spirit of John at the fishing hole, I started to look at the lights floating around the apartment a little differently. I started to listen a little more carefully to the whispers. Yet, I need to explain an important piece of this puzzle, as I believe it pertains to my gifts. Prior to my head injury, I could see colors. It was a gift that I have had most of my life, but did not realize it was not normal until 2007, when I started massage school. In school, we had many discussions about energy and how it is represented by different colors. In Traditional Chinese Medicine, a practitioner could look at the pallor of someone's skin, or tongue, and determine what energy system needed balancing. The instructors of the class said that some people could see the energy colors. Now, I don't remember if I asked the question of my instructor or just thought it, but I remember thinking about how I saw blue and yellow around the trees. I always assumed that this was my artist's eye, interpreting the composition that I would paint.

As I progressed in school, I realized that I was seeing colors around the individuals that I was massaging. One day, I asked if there were meanings assigned to the colors, other than what we had learned in acupressure and our Traditional Chinese Medicine studies. I remember what the instructor told me. She said, "That interpretation is unique to you. It isn't about what meaning I assign to that color. It is about the meaning you assign to it." This opened up a whole new way of looking at my clients. For one client, green in an area of their field may have signified envy, whereas, in another client the color signaled toxicity of tissue. Throughout my schooling, I only noticed this gift while working in massage, or working on various art pieces.

My accident changed this gift in more ways than one. Or rather, the accident made me fully aware that I was seeing more than color. I was hearing, seeing, feeling and smelling energetic and spiritual beings all of the time. More than that, I had already been communicating with them through thoughts and words. Although I was not completely conscious of this then, I developed a certainty that I was returning to a gift with which I was born. At some point in my youth, I repressed this gift because I was afraid to practice it out of fear of being bullied more than I was. I would have to explain to people that I was not living in a fantasy world, any more than they were. It was the accident that flipped the switch back on for me to see. However, it was the experience with Cally that allowed me to be open to receiving more information this way. Cally completely accepted me and didn't question what I saw, because she saw it too. She didn't think I was crazy because she would have to put herself in the same category.

In the following two months, I did not see any more complete images of these spiritual beings. At least, I am not aware that I was seeing them, though I began to question that after November. For, it was the Wednesday before Thanksgiving when I saw John again. I was headed to work for my shift before going up to the cabin to hunt with my father-in-law. Although I was not sure I wanted to go, I felt that I needed to go and be there. This was something I had been doing for the past 7 years with John. I felt that I needed to do it, as Jack was up there without his son for the first year in I don't know how long. John loved deer hunting and loved sharing it with me- from the first year we were married. So, it was on my way to work that morning when those lights and whispers changed into people with voices.

Anyway, I was driving to work in the Jeep when I smelled this Old Spice™ deodorant John used to wear. Then, I felt him. I don't know how to explain it, but I knew it was John before I even looked over to find him sitting in the passenger seat watching me. I could feel his presence like anyone could feel a hug. I imagine all couples feel that tangible connection with their significant other- their soulmate. When I looked at him, I blinked and looked again, trying to not be distracted from driving.

"Hi Dear!" he said from his spot.

"Am I imagining this? I haven't had my coffee yet."

His laughter seemed to bounce around in the Jeep as he shook his head. "No, you aren't imagining it. I'm really here."

"How? Why now?"

"I wanted to thank you for going hunting," he began. "I know your heart aches and that you are doing it for my dad."

"Well, I am. But, I think I have to do it for me, too." As I said it, a tear slid down my cheek. I knew this was real, but was afraid it wasn't. Plus, I was worried that he would be gone if I blinked again.

"I know you have questions."

I confessed that I did with a nod of my head.

"I can answer some of them, but you will need to figure out the rest," John explained.

The first thing I needed to know was about the accident. The report from witnesses was that John was slumped over the steering wheel when he passed the first two cars. "Did you have a stroke?" I asked, unsure of why I felt this was important. I had read the autopsy and knew that he was legally drunk. Although I never said anything to them, I was very angry with Ann and Jeff for lying to me about how much John had been drinking that day. The night of his accident, I knew they were lying to my repeated question. Then, to have Jeff accuse me of lying to Brooke turned the knife even more. But, knowing he was legally drunk did nothing to erase my certainty that something else caused the accident.

"Yes, I believe I did." He said. Then, he made a simple request, "don't be angry with my mom and Jeff. They have their own grief to process."

"Have I said anything? I know that." I could not believe he knew what I was thinking. "Did you know that something was wrong?"

"Yes."

"Why didn't you go to the doctor?"

"We were dealing with your issue. Plus, I didn't want you worrying about me."

"So, you would have me going through my life alone? Damnit John! This is unfair to me and to Brooke."

"Yeah, but none of her actions are your fault either. Bill is right. She made her choice to run away. She made her choice to hate herself and you because of this. Don't worry about her. She will be fine."

Brooke had run away to Georgia in October after I kicked her out. Her disrespect for me had increased and she was behaving and acting out against me. On my birthday in early October, Cally and I decided to make a trip up north. When Cally came in, she gave me a bottle of wine and a card. Brooke saw it on the table and said, "Oh yeah, Happy Birthday!" Cally vented all the way up north about how she couldn't believe that Brooke forgot my birthday and didn't even acknowledge it until she saw me reading Cally's card. She was very angry with Brooke- more so than I.

"It's hard for me to believe that she will be fine," I said. "I feel so inadequate in dealing with her. You get her."

"You do, too. It's just that you are both alike in many ways. You've changed though."

By this time, I was sobbing and trying to get composed.

"Why did you have to die?"

"Because I am the only person who you would trust to bring you the message I have for you." He said it so gently, like he was trying to protect me.

"What do you mean?"

"Toni, I had to die so that you could do what you were meant to do in this lifetime."

"What?" I asked again.

"You see me, right?" he asked.

"Yes."

"You hear me?"

Again, I answered affirmatively.

"You feel me, smell me, and could actually touch my body. You know I am here."

"Yes, I know you are here. But, why? How?"

"I had to be the one to tell you that this is real. And, you need to be prepared to see, feel, hear, smell and know more. There is going to be more coming to you and I am here to help you learn how to work with it."

"It?" I asked.

"Yes, your gifts. You are not crazy. I apologize if I made you feel like you were," he explained. "I know, now, that you are seeing Spirit. You are a messenger."

"John, I don't understand."

"I know. And, I do not have a lot of time to explain it to you now." He reached to touch my cheek, wiping a tear away, as he used to do. "There will be more like me coming to you. And you need to trust yourself to work with them."

"What?"

"I love you and for now, you need to know that you are protected by many, many angels."

"I love you too. But, I don't know what you mean."

"Just watch for signs and trust yourself to know their meaning. I am always here for you."

"OK. Will I be able to see you all the time?"

"No. But, there will be others- Angels, Archangels, Ghosts, Spirit animals and guides. You will see it all- the good and the bad."

I felt this urgency to keep him there, but I knew he was about to disappear. "What are you?"

"I am one of the good guys," he said with a smile. "But, I have to go for now. I love you and always will."

"I love you too." Before I could ask another question, he disappeared. He was gone from my sight and the essence that was his was gone. I felt this relief and lightness, but also the sorrow of not having him.

The conversation only took up a few minutes of my drive, but it seemed to occupy most of my morning. As I pulled into the parking lot at work, I heard "quit your blubbering" in my left ear. Then, I felt a kiss on my right cheek. He hadn't left me. He was still there.

When I got to the cabin that night, it was dark and cold. There was snow earlier in the week, which presented perfect hunting for deer. My father-in-law was there alone when I pulled into the drive. John was there, too. You could feel his presence. At one point, Jack even said to me, "Yeah, I've had moments when I can see him standing there and had to do a double-take." To hear him admit this was reassuring to me, as I would have never expected him to make this confession to me. Yet, in those moments where it was just he and I, it was so appropriate. It was the truth that it was real, as this man of few words would not make up stories about his dead son. He would not hand me a load of crap to make me feel better. Not only would it be like rubbing salt in my wounds, it would hurt him as well.

In the quiet of the woods that weekend, there were moments when I felt completely alone for the first time in 11 months. Not even the crows disturbed the quietness that surrounded me. It was soul-stirring, as so many noises had been bombarding me for so long. I had forgotten what it was like to hear my heart beating. Even though I sat in the woods and felt alone, I knew I wasn't. I knew that this silence was meant to help me just calm myself and know that the whispering and lights and sensational chaos that I had been feeling did not have to be chaotic at all. My first lesson of understanding was there in that stand of pine trees.

After Thanksgiving, the days flew by to Christmas. The week after Christmas, I received a call from Brooke telling me that she wanted to come home. Her situation in Georgia escalated to a volatile existence of men, experimentation with drugs and jobless homelessness. I agreed that she could return home and that I would help her do so, if she agreed to living by my rules. I paid for her vehicle to be fixed in Georgia. I paid for her gas to get home. I paid for a night in a hotel.

And, I told her to get in her vehicle and drive, sending her the directions that I had printed off of Map Quest. Her instructions were to come to my apartment and wait there until I got off work. She decided she was going to go to her Aunt's house in Boyceville, Wisconsin and ignore my directive, in hopes that her aunt would allow her to live there with her.

When she finally did get to my apartment, I told her my rules and had a contract for her to sign. I was not going to support her and pay her way. I expected her to get a job. I worked very hard to keep myself in the apartment and I was not going to give her any handouts. I had shown her compassion and done all that I could to help her, while she had repeatedly disrespected me. Although I understood that this girl was still grieving and had so much damage already ingrained in her before the death of her father, it wasn't anything that I could fix. But, it would have hurt me too much to not try to help. I do have to mention that everyone in her family believed that they had the right answer and impressed upon her (albeit, unknowingly to them) that I was wrong. I received a lot of criticism from a few individuals and was told what they would do. Yet, they were not in my situation and they were not stepping up to the plate to take over. If this was their child, I am not sure that their decisions would have been any different than mine. I am pretty sure that she would not have been turned away to live on the street, or in her car, as Brooke was by her family. I chose to make her accountable for her decisions, offering her the choice to respect me and my rules, while living under my roof. Her decision to not live by my rules was her decision to leave, every time.

After she moved back in, Brooke enrolled in beauty school and started in February. I was happy she was going to school for something and helped her apply for loans. Legally, I was not her parent, so this was quite the task. We had to get Theresa involved. Again, I paid for her start-up costs. Brooke's tab with me was up over $10K over less than a year. She was in school for less than a month and decided that she was going to move out and live with her high school friend's family. She didn't like my rules, me, or evidently anything I had done. I had worked two jobs for 5 years, allowing John to graduate from college and me to graduate from massage school. At the time, she made it clear that she felt she was entitled to free room and board and no rules. This started a process of Brooke living with her Mom, me, and other strangers-bouncing around like a golf ball on pavement. Each time she came and went, she ripped another shred of flesh from my heart, wounding me, until I realized that there was nothing I could do to make her forgive me for NOT being the one who died in March of 2009.

About the time Brooke got home, I met with Tim, John's friend from school. He lived in Las Vegas, but came home regularly to visit with his family. I met him at a local bar. The Old Saloon was located in downtown New Richmond and owned by a couple that grew up with John's crew. When Tim came into town, at least one of our nights was spent there. With all the teenage drama that Brooke brought, I must confess I needed a beer.

That night, Jill and Dave were not there. Wisconsin had just passed a law prohibiting smoking in the bars and Tim was a smoker. At one point, he went outside to the back of the bar to have a cigarette. While he was gone, I sat at the bar. I turned to face forward and noticed an older man sitting next to me, drinking a beer. I smiled and nodded at him.

"How are you today?" he asked me. His voice was a rich baritone spiked with a German accent.

"I am good," I told him.

"Don't let your daughter walk on you," he said.

The comment threw me off a bit, as I had not said a whole lot to Tim, other than telling him that I had paid for Brooke to come home and that she was driving me to drink.

"I'm sorry," he apologized, "I couldn't help but hear she's been causing you concern."

"Yes, I feel like I cannot win with her," I sort of laughed while I said it.

"Don't you worry, she will come around. She is just missing her father."

"Yes. So am I." I wanted to move to lighter conversation with this stranger. It was odd that he knew about things that I had not discussed with Tim, so I asked him, "Am I detecting a German accent?"

"Ah, you have a good ear!" the man laughed, seeming happy that I identified the uniqueness of his words. "Do you speak German?"

"No. I only know a couple phrases, which were part of my husband's jokes."

"Let me hear it!"

"Ich bin grössen die hose," I said. My understanding of this phrase was the one my husband had given me. Loosely translated, it meant "I am big in the pants."

The man roared with laughter. I explained to him the story of Brooke's German class in Catholic school and John sending her back to the teacher with that phrase. I was laughing while telling it and had not noticed that Tim had returned to sit next to me. When I finished telling the story, I noticed Tim was looking oddly at me and he said, "Who are you talking to?"

The bartender stated that he had been wondering the same thing and when I turned to ask the man for his name, there was nobody sitting there. The beer the man had been drinking was not there. In fact, it appeared that nobody had been sitting there and that I had indeed been talking to myself and laughing like a lunatic. Embarrassed, I just shook my head and retold the story I was telling to the non-existent man at the bar. I didn't explain to either of them that there was a man sitting there and I'm pretty sure they thought I was crazy. We just moved on to other topics and I acted as if nothing unusual had occurred. Later, I pondered this discussion with the man. I knew his name was Heinrich, even though I had never asked him.

From that day forward, the whispers became words. The colors became actual people and angels. And, I was coming to the realization that I was not going to turn it off. I would have to figure out why this gift was now mine and what I needed to do to work with it. Then, how does one go about finding a teacher for something like this? It's not like you put out a classified ad! I imagined it would read something like:

"Instructor wanted! Non-crazy, sober, female needs instructor to explain the voices in her head and the hallucinations she sees in a holistic manner. No drugs or weapons necessary. Just have knowledge of metaphysical practices and a willingness to not commit me to a mental institution. References and experience required. "

When I spoke to Cally about it, she laughed about the silliness of taking out an advertisement for an intuitive teacher. However, we both knew that there were classes I could take to help. She suggested I start with June, the owner of the massage school. But, I had reservations about doing that. It was quite strange for me to admit that at the time. However, I decided to take some classes from people in the community that were advertising classes. In addition, I found and read some material on mediums. Regardless, it was obvious to me that I had to do something quickly. The old man in the bar seemed to open a gate to the Spirit world for me and I could not close it. Plus, it was obvious that I could not always tell the difference between a ghost and a real person- which made me wonder how many times other people had observed me talking to someone that wasn't there.

Chapter 14

Ringing In Another Year

The beginning of 2010 marked the anniversary of my head injury. I allowed it to slip past without notice. It was the first year in ten years that I had not determined a resolution. In the back of my mind, I resolved to get through another year without John. But, I had already gotten through nine months without him. **I had enough determination to get through another year.** I had some great friends and family that helped me. I stayed home alone and occasionally went out with Cally, or went to see Tara, or any number of friends and relatives.

The personality change that I had from my head injury allowed me to handle my husband's death and kept me calmer at my full-time job. Yet, the Spirit that I saw and heard continuously, made it difficult to concentrate on the phone conversations. I worked for a company that administered benefits for **long-term** care insurance. There were days when Spirit would be talking through the phone to me at the same time as the actual caller. Then, you add the cluster bomb of employees with a variety of issues and I was hard- pressed to stay on task. I felt the emotional turmoil of everyone else, but held a continued numbness with **my own**.

At the end of January, I went to Cally's 36th birthday party. This girl was beautiful to the core and I loved her like a sister. I was so blessed to have her there when John died. I was able to tell her about everything I was experiencing and she was completely supportive. I think she relied on me in the same way. That is not to say I did not have several supportive friends, as Tara, Chris and several of my work and school friends were understanding and right there if I needed them. But, I worked at my full-time job with Cally. I went to school and massaged with her. She lived within 20 miles of me. **Not to mention**, we just clicked. There are things that I knew about her that I will take to my grave, just as she knew my secrets.

As with many of Cally's parties, there was a lot of drinking. Although I like to have a cocktail, or a glass of wine on occasion, the current state of my **psyche** dictated that I go easy on anything that would render me useless. In the past nine months, there were many times when I wanted to go into a bottle and stay in a state of obliviousness. Yet, the thought of losing my control to alcohol seemed irresponsible to myself and Brooke. I vowed somewhere that I would not drink to try to wipe out the emotional pain of losing John. In addition, I was completely aware that I would have no control over my gift if I was not in control of myself. So, it was with this intention that I got into the party van at her parent's house and went bar hopping with her.

To be honest, I am not sure how many drinks Cally had. However, I had noticed at previous parties that her tolerance for alcohol was very small. She seemed to get intoxicated quickly. We had talked on several occasions about it. On the night of her party, she got very drunk with her mother, sister, brother and most of her friends. But, she was so far gone that I became angry. From our earlier discussions, Cally and I had discussed what could be wrong with her system that she would get completely hammered after only a couple drinks. Our anatomy, physiology and pathology courses in school led us to believe that she had something going on in her liver and lymphatic system. She had promised me she would have that checked before having her tonsils removed in the next couple weeks. When I was in the bathroom with her, trying to get her pants up, she slurred, "Yep, my liver is fucked."

"What?" I asked her in a stern comeback.

"You heard me!"

"Cally, pull up you pants and stop drinking!"

"Are you mad at me? Don't yell at me!"

As I stood there in the bathroom, I noticed the yellowness of her skin and eyes. I felt a hand on my shoulder.

When I turned to look, I saw this beautiful angel. I blinked and she was still there. Her wings looked like pillows of cotton puffs with light pink and purple tips, her hair curled in a fire of red and golden orange around those wings, and her eyes were like oceans of turquoise, green, and blue. "There is no point in arguing with a drunkard," she said into my head. "She knows what the drinking is doing to her."

"You be quiet, Caron!" Cally slurred at me, as if I had said it. "I don't need you reminding me of my liver."

"Are you talking to me?" I asked her. She was looking at me, but called me Caron.

"Noooo!" she said, leaning forward and stumbling into me. "I'm talking to Caron! You two are in cahoots."

"Damnit Cally! Just pull up your pants!" I said, before I left her in the hands of another friend that had come to help her. I left her in the bathroom and went out to have another Coke. Caron seemed to disappear as quickly as she came. But, Cally's dad noticed me coming out of the bathroom.

"I think we're done bar hopping," he said.

"Yep, I would agree."

Within an hour, we all piled into the van and were on our way back to the ranch home of Cally's parents. Most of the party-goers were going in and finding a place to crash. I decided to just go home. I was extremely tired and completely sober. So, I drove the 30 miles home at three in the morning, assuring her father I was fine. I think he knew that.

As I reached the highway from the country road, the car filled with a bright light. I looked around to see where it was coming from, and Caron was sitting next to me. "I must be tired!" I laughed to myself.

"You know I am really here," Caron said. "You can stop pretending like you think you are seeing things."

"I would if I didn't feel like I was making this up in my injured brain."

"Hog wash! You know I am real!"

"Let's just say that I choose the path of least resistance for my own sanity."

Her colors intensified to something that was more blinding than the sun. She was so beautiful that it was painful to look at her. But, I did. I was mesmerized. Plus, her brightness made it hard to see outside.

"Toni, slow down and watch the road, or you are going to hit that deer ahead."

Just as I let my foot off the accelerator, I turned my head and saw the bright orange eyes coming from the ditch. I honked my horn and it turned in the other direction. Although I avoided hitting the deer, it took all my willpower not to look at Caron. "Can you dim yourself a bit? You make it hard to see the road."

"Sorry," she said, turning herself down to a soft glow.

"Do you appear like this all the time? Or, can you change your form?"

"Most of the time, I come with my wings because that is how people think angels should look."

"So, do you really have wings?"

"Actually, we move by thought and can be everywhere at once. But, yes, angels have wings. That is how you will differentiate us from other Spirit beings." .

"Yeah, I guess I have seen the difference."

"Even the fallen angels have wings," Caron said.

"So, you are not all fallen?"

"No." It was a simple answer, but it implied more to me. Caron just let it sink in and seemed to be waiting for me to say something. When I looked ahead and continued to drive, she started to hum. This forced me to look at her, because when she did this, the sound was like a choir in the car; her one voice added to hundreds of others. It was magnificent and beautiful and utterly distracting.

"Oh my God! Am I going to die?" I asked, suddenly wondering if this beauty was a gentle angel of death. Why else would I be hearing choirs of angels? Maybe I had already died?

The choir stopped as quickly as it started. "Not right now, Dear," she assured me. "You are much too needed at this time in your world."

"What?" I asked. What was she talking about? I was one person with limited talent. What did she mean by "my world"? They were just thoughts in my head, as I didn't want to offend her by asking them aloud.

"You have many talents," she interrupted my thought, "but the ones that are most important you are just now learning to use again. And, your world is this present time on this planet."

"What am I learning to use again?"

"Your gifts to discern Spirit. You will remember more soon."

"Remembering?"

"You don't remember that you used to see us when you were a child. Toni, you are a messenger, like me."

"I don't have rainbows blowing out my a--," I stopped myself before saying it, but Caron started laughing. Her laughter was musical, too. "How am I like you? I have a life on this plane," she explained. "But, you are meant to bring peace to others through your work on your plane, just as you have for millions of years. Plus, I do not have rainbows blowing out my ass, as you say."

"So, why are you here talking to me?"

"John was busy."

"John? My husband?"

"Yes. Besides, you wouldn't believe you could see other things if we sent him again."

"So, what is he busy doing in his afterlife?"

"He is fishing with his grandfather and your father."

Maybe I was just tired? Or, maybe I was just angry because my dead husband had someone to go fishing with in January. Regardless, I could feel the sarcastic resentment coming up out of my mouth before I could stop it. "Gee," I said, "I'm so glad that his fishing trip took precedence over my ride to crazy town with an angel named Caron. I'm glad he is having so much fun, now that he left me alone to deal with everything!"

She didn't get angry with me. She didn't disappear. She seemed to hug me without even moving. "We know you feel alone, but you aren't. We know this is hard because you loved him and feel that loss. And, we know that you are afraid of these gifts because of what happened in your earlier years. But, I assure you that we are here, you are protected, and we love you very much. He loved you enough to let go."

I had tears rolling down my cheeks, but I managed to ask her again, "Why are you here?"

"I need to tell you that we are here to help you. We are here to answer questions. Ask and you will receive answers."

"So, who is Heinrich? Was he a ghost or an angel?"

"He is more of a spirit than a ghost. He isn't stuck there. He just chooses to be there."

"Is he on the same plane as you?"

"Sort of," Caron answered vaguely.

I thought for a minute before I asked her, "Did you come tonight for me, or Cally?"

The angel paused for a moment, like she was unsure how to answer. "I came more for you tonight, but I am usually assigned to Cally."

"Like a guardian?"

"Exactly!" she exclaimed. "I knew you understood."

"I've seen you before today." It wasn't a question. I knew that I had seen her at another time. I could not figure out where, but I was positive.

"You have seen me. It has been a while since you acknowledged my presence."

"When?"

"That is not important at this time. But, you know me."

In writing this part of my story, I realized that there were many questions that were answered during this drive that I never asked out loud. In fact, I do not even remember all of the questions that were answered, other than knowing that there was a lot packed into that 20 minutes. As the lights of New Richmond came into view, I realized that I had missed most of the drive. I wondered how I got to this point without paying attention. "Did I stop at 4 corners?" I wondered in my head.

"Yes, you stopped," Caron answered, as if I had asked her the question out loud. Then, as if it were a whisper in my head, "You do not even have to ask your questions out loud. All you have to do is think it."

"I'm beginning to understand that," I said out loud this time.

"We'll teach you, my dear," Caron said. "Just ask us when you have questions."

"All right. Will this come easier?"

"It already has. You saw John, Heinrich and me. You have seen Timothy and your father."

"Can I make this less traumatic for myself? Like, can I turn it off before I go out?"

"We'll help you set up working boundaries. For now, we will do some blocking. You will figure it out."

Pulling into the driveway of my apartment, Caron told me to rest and go inside. She promised that I was protected and that everything would be fine. At that moment, I believed her because it was easier than not believing. I did not think I could prove the reality of this experience to anyone, but I felt it to my inner core. It was enough at that moment, because I was too tired to make it any more than a visit from an angel.

For some reason, I never mentioned Caron to anyone. It was in the following week that Cally had her tonsils out and I didn't see her for a week or more. We talked on the phone and never mentioned the drunken confrontation. I am not entirely sure that she remembered having it with me. Yet, I gave myself the opportunity to process what I saw on my own by not saying anything. Further, it allowed me to tune in to the multitudes of angels that were coming and going in my day, as well as other spirits. They were everywhere!

One night, I was sitting in my living room at home just watching the spirits come and go. There was not any specific way they arrived, or left. Some just appeared, while others came through the wall, or the door. There were so many of them that I started to wonder if my apartment was a portal to the other side, like the train portal in the Harry Potter Series. "Next stop: Toni's train to crazy town!" I joked to myself.

"I told you I was sorry for saying that to you," John's voice came from the chair next to me. The cat was on my lap and he got up, sniffing the air as if he knew John was there. "Hello Nova!" I saw John scratch his ears.

He actually startled me, just appearing next to me like that. On this particular night, he was wearing a long robe. It was bright white, with this iridescent green running through it. He was beautiful.

"So, you made a diamond out of my ashes?" he asked, with a chuckle.

"Two," I corrected him.

In August, I was outside smoking a cigarette at work with a bunch of people talking about the remainder of John's ashes. Someone mentioned that they were going to make diamonds with the ashes of their father. I was not aware that you could do anything like that with the cremated remains of a human. I did some research on it and decided to spend way too much money doing just that. I sent an eight ounce jar of John's ashes to a place outside of Chicago. In February, his remains had already been heated to extract carbon and were now being applied to enormous amounts of pressure for the next 4-6 months.

"You cannot give one to Brooke. She is not ready."

"I have already decided that I am not giving her one for a long time. She may not get one until I die, with her attitude being what it is," I told him.

"There will come a time when you will realize that all of the things you are hanging onto are not giving you any comfort."

"I think I am realizing that already," I told him. "Nothing is bringing you back to this time and place. Even though I can see and hear you, I don't know that you are really here. I still question if it is really possible for me to be speaking to you."

"Thomas, I have no holes in my hands that you can probe," he laughed.

"Really? A biblical reference?"

"It applies here."

"You are not Jesus!"

"No, but he is pretty cool. So is your Dad, by the way."

"I wouldn't know. He died when I was six." I said it and felt the hurt it gave me. I didn't remember my father. Although, I secretly hoped that he approved of John, I had no idea if he would have liked him, if he was alive. "Why doesn't he come and talk to me?"

"He does. But, you cannot hear him."

"Why is that?"

"You blocked him when you were in high school. But, you have talked to him since then. Remember?"

"I think so. It was in my massage with Cally before we went to **Flippin**, Arkansas."

"Yes."

At that moment, I felt him there, too. I don't know how I knew it was my father, as my memories of him alive had faded. He'd been gone most of my life. Yet, I just knew he was there. I could not see him in the crowd of Spirit, but I could feel him there. "So, I still cannot hear him?"

"Give yourself some time. He's quite protective of you and is here."

"Okay. So, why are you here?" I asked.

The buzzing in the room seemed to stop. I looked away from John's face to see my question caused all sound and movement to stop. Suddenly, I felt like I had just made a scene in a quiet restaurant and everyone turned to look at me. All eyes were turned toward me and all sound had stopped. As I looked around the room, I realized that I could have been asking that question of any one of these beings. Maybe they were all going to answer?

John cleared his throat, as he did a hundred times when he was alive. I decided it was his habit when he was anxious about something. Some people sniffed, some tapped their foot, and John cleared his throat needlessly. "Word is out," John began, "that you are accepting your gift again. The angels are here to protect you, as am I. Your father is here to make sure we do our job well enough."

I started to laugh before I asked, "From what? What are you protecting me from?"

"Toni, you do not only see angels! You see spirit from all sides, all planes, and many levels. There are some entities in here that you are not ready to take on alone."

"Like demons?"

"Yes."

"Not ready? You mean I will take them on at some time."

"Never alone, as you have an angel posse I have yet to see with anyone else. But, you will be encountering things and you are still vulnerable."

"Why am I vulnerable?" I asked, a bit perplexed by the fact that he thought I was prepared for angels and other things, but not demons.

"Because, this still freaks you out. You are still remembering your gifts."

"John," I began, "why do you think I call in angels when I work? Why do you think I set the intention for protection? Do you not know that I realize evil comes in many forms?"

"Then, tell me, what in this room is evil?" It was a challenge.

"As I did not call you here, I could assume all of you are evil. For all I know, you could be Satan in a disguise. But, I can tell you with certainty that you are not. The reason I can tell you this, is because I protected my home with God and his

Archangels. If it does not come in the name of God, it cannot be here. I trust that, so I know you are not Satan. "

I think my answer surprised him. Yet, I believe that was what allowed me to let go of some of my resistance to my gifts. For the second time in 24 years, my father appeared in front of me with Timothy, my guardian angel. My father had this look on his face that I had seen in my own reflection and the faces of my siblings. He had a sarcastic smirk on his face that said, "Yep, that's my daughter! She's got this."

Chapter 15

Building Boundaries

February of 2010 came in abnormally warm. Although fifty degree temperatures in February were not unheard of in Western Wisconsin and Minnesota, they were very rare. In the beginning of the month, Brooke started beauty school and the ground hog did not see his shadow. I continued learning from the angels and spirits that showed up everywhere. One of the most important things I learned was how to discern the difference between spirit and real people in public places. This was divine intervention if I ever saw it! I'd been spending the last few months trying to convince myself that I was not crazy. If I was talking to myself in a grocery store and I had to convince someone that I was actually speaking with Spirit, I'm sure they would have committed me to a psychiatric ward.

I was wondering through Wal-Mart in New Richmond, just trying to kill some time before going home to my empty apartment, when this new found knowledge forged a personal boundary that I cataloged into my code of ethics. I was in the kitchen gadgets when a spirit came up to me and said, "Hey, I need you." This man was an older gentleman wearing work boots and jeans. He had a flannel shirt on and a beautiful head of silver hair.

As I knew that he could hear me if I spoke in my head, I asked him silently, "What do you want?"

"My wife's here spending my money on stupid shit and I need you to tell her to stop it."

"Why should I?"

"Because it's my money!" he yelled in my head.

"First of all, you're dead. Second, it is no longer your money. Wisconsin is a shared property state, so all that was yours is now hers," I informed him. "And, finally, it is not my place to tell her anything in regards to how she is spending her money!"

Just then, an older woman came into the aisle, pushing a loaded shopping cart. The cart was full to the brim. The expression on her face was a mixture of lost sadness and anticipation. I knew she was alive and I knew it was his wife, as he made disapproving noises when she picked up a vegetable peeler. "What the hell does she need that for? She has a perfectly good paring knife at home!"

"Hey, Tightwad," I raised my voice in my head with disapproval, "I'm surprised she didn't stab you in your sleep with that paring knife! Have you ever peeled a potato with a knife? It's a pain in the ass with arthritis, which she obviously has!"

"Say something to her!"

198

"All right," I said to him. Then, with the sweetest disposition I could muster, I said to the woman, "Ma'am, I could not help but notice that you selected this potato peeler." I pointed to the item in her cart.

"Yes," she said, with a question in her eyes.

"I found this one to be more comfortable to hold," selecting a more expensive peeler from the rack. I went on to explain, "I have rheumatoid arthritis and peeling potatoes is a pain in the hands. This one is so much easier to use."

The eyes of the ghost became very dark with anger. However, the woman's eyes lit up. "Thank you, Dear!" the woman said with appreciation. "My late husband was very frugal and I have been having issues with my hands for years. I decided to make things easier."

"Good for you!" I said. "I'm sure your late husband would want you to make things easier for yourself."

The ghost was upset with me, but realized that his wife was suffering. I could tell he wanted to lay into me. Yet, his wife's next words changed his expression, "I highly doubt that, Dear. I was being nice when I said he was frugal. He did not see the need to make things easy."

I did not say anything in response. I just nodded a little, which seemed to encourage her to continue. "His grandchildren were afraid of him, so they never came over. Whenever I wanted to do something nice for the children, he would become resentful of me spending money on anything. He grew up poor and worked hard on his farm. That man was very good at turning a profit, but refused to spend that money on anything."

"So, he struggled with money?" I asked, before I could stop myself.

"Oh no!" the woman laughed a little. "But, he died with piles of it everywhere. He struggled with spending money!"

"Well, I hope he left you well cared for." It was a statement that I hoped would end the conversation.

"He did. I have been saving part of my allowance for 57 years and investing it and buying myself little things that he wouldn't notice. When he died last year, I retired. My IRA will keep me living comfortable for the next 20 years, or until I die. His money is going to put his grandchildren through college."

"She is spending her own money," the man said, all the anger gone from his spirit. "I had no idea she was doing that!" He had grabbed her hand and was holding it gently, looking at the arthritic fingers with a different expression.

"I just couldn't let my children and grandchildren think that he did not love them. He did, in his own way. Just as he loved me," the woman said.

"Well, I'm glad you are doing things that feel right to you," I said.

The man asked me to tell her that he was there and that he loved her. But, I didn't have to do that, as she already knew he loved her. I told him as much. As she left the aisle, he went with her. Somehow, his energy had softened.

I turned to continue my own shopping and there were three other people behind me, clamoring to be heard.

"You need to talk to my daughter!" one said.

Another spoke over the first, "Can you see me?"

Then, the third said, "Go over and tell my brother that he needs to stop doing drugs."

"Stop it!" I said. "If you want me to speak to your loved ones, you need to find a way to get them to come to me! Not everyone believes or accepts this! Now, leave me alone, or I will have Michael, or Uriel, take you over where you cannot come back." For some reason, I knew that Michael and Uriel could do that, even though I had no clue if they would do it if I told them to do so. But, it seemed to do the trick, as all three of them left me alone and went to their respective family members. I realized I did not want to ever approach anyone without being invited. It felt wrong to me; an invasion of privacy. I thought about how I would feel if a medium came up to me, started reading my energy field and the people in it with me. To me, that was personal and private.

I finished my shopping and went home. I was kind of exhausted. But, I had started creating the boundaries which would define how I would work. I would never go up to anyone in a public place and talk to them about their deceased loved ones. As I said, not everyone believes in Spirit, or an afterlife. Not everyone is ready to speak about their loss. Their healing had to come from their own decisions.

At some point that month, I went to a psychic fair in Hudson. I felt put upon by a bunch of vampires sucking my energy out. I walked in the door and could feel these men and women scanning me. I walked by the booths to hear some of the conversations going on with people receiving readings and wondered how these people were successful, when their surface energy was masked in trickery. I did a loop around the room, finding a booth selling oracle cards. I bought a deck. I went by this booth of psychic women and one of them jumped in front of me stating, "Wow, you have an intense energy field! Let me give you a reading. It's only thirty dollars today."

"No thank you," I said moving further down the line. By this time, I was perspiring and extremely hot. I didn't like the feeling. I do not remember if I agreed to meet her there, or if we happened upon each other, but I met up with one of my instructors from school, Chris.

Chris must of seen how flushed I was, as she came up and brushed down my back quickly, as if wiping off a bug. "Create a mirrored bubble and put yourself in the middle," she told me.

I did as I was told, quickly feeling the effects of that mirror. "June used to tell us that in class," I remembered.

"Yup," Chris confirmed. "As those people scan you, they only see their own reflection in the mirror. They cannot run your energy the way they were just now."

"Nobody in here feels good," I stated. "I wanted to get a reading, but have never had one and didn't know what to expect."

"I just got here. Let's go around again and I will tell you who I would go to." So, we walked together, stopping at tables to look at things being sold. There was a guy with singing bowls doing healing sessions. Someone was doing aura photos and energy healings. There were a couple tarot readers and people that just said they were psychic. Chris would point out things that she liked and didn't like about certain vendors. When we got to the psychic trio with the $30 readings, Chris told me to keep my eyes straight ahead and keep walking.

After we had come full circle, Chris turned me to a table where a girl was doing "art readings", stating, "She has the best energy in this place right now. I think I'm going to find out more about what she is offering."

"What's an art reading?" Chris asked the young woman.

"Well, you ask a question and I will draw an answer for you."

"Okay, do you have time to do a reading?"

The woman had a sign-up sheet. Chris put her name on the list and I put mine after hers. She told Chris to come back in about fifteen minutes, so we went back to watch the singing bowl treatments going on at the far end of the room. While Chris had her reading, I looked at some more angel cards. The singing bowl thing looked cool, but I didn't have the money for a session.

When I went to have my session, I didn't have a question to ask the woman. So, I said, "What do I need to know?"

She sat for a minute and pondered the question. Then, she drew three things on the paper with watercolor pencils. She finished drawing, then, as she wet a small paint brush, she explained what she was shown. The first thing she mentioned was travel to India. But, she said that it was past-life travel. The image was a simple drawing of the Taj Mahal. She stated that she felt that I would travel in this lifetime, but that I had to find happiness first. The second image was of mountains. Her interpretation was that I had mountains to climb right now, but that I would do it and have much to tell about my journeys. The third image was that of a heart that was scarred over several times, which she felt signified future love, as my broken heart would heal. Chris nodded and I thanked her, paying her the required amount.

I left with my painting and Chris behind me. "You know," Chris said, as we walked out of the hotel where the fair was being held, "I see you doing art readings."

"Really?" I kind of laughed when I said that, as I had thought that this was something I could do. "But, I cannot draw."

"Sure you can! I've seen the paintings you have done."

"That's funny. The reason why I came here in the first place was because I was hoping to see the Angel Lady here."

"Toni, you can do that too."

"I cannot draw people!" I insisted, "Not like that, anyway."

"Start practicing. I bet it would come to you easily."

Chris had to go and I was heading home for the afternoon. For the whole drive home, I could not stop thinking about how great it would be if I could draw what I saw every day. What if I could draw people's guides and angels, like the Angel Lady? What if I could give art readings? I mind raced to other ideas. What if I could create my own angel oracle deck? What if I just gave angel readings and worked with that energy?

As I pulled into my drive way, I thought about how my family and friends outside of school would perceive me if I told them I see dead people. Would they think I was making it all up? Would they think I was lying? Would they tell me I'm crazy?   I opened the door to my apartment as I thought, "Who the hell cares what everyone else thinks? You are not crazy. Plus, it is not your job to prove anything exists."

It was not my job to prove that angels and demons were real. It was not my job to prove that I was not crazy. I did not have to prove to anyone that my experience was real. The only person who needed to believe in my gifts was me. If I shared my gifts with integrity and for the highest good of others, then I was being true to myself. I didn't have to be someone I was not anymore. I didn't have to prove anything to anyone. "Who cares what other people think?" John's words rang in my memory.

Most people go through the death of a loved one never seeing the blessings that come from losing someone for whom they cared so deeply. In general, everyone experiences a traumatic experience that changes them. For me, I had two personal traumas that changed me in miraculous ways. Although these two incidents were completely separate from each other, the blessings of each of them were codependent.

Neither incident would have impacted me the same without the other. I had quickly realized the blessings of my head injury in dealing with John's death. But, it took me longer to recognize the blessing in his death, even though I knew it was there. I would not have had the understanding of the gift he gave me in death, if I had never had the head injury. I could not have one without the other.

One of the things John was really smart about was the fact that we always made choices. Once we made a decision and executed that decision, there was no turning back. The best example he ever gave was when he was talking to Brooke about an individual's sexual preference. Brooke was telling us that her friend, who was openly dating a person of the same sex, had started dating someone of the opposite sex. She explained that her friend said that nothing ever happened in the same-sex relationship and that she was not a lesbian anymore.

John explained to Brooke that her friend had openly introduced the girl she was dating as her girlfriend. On more than one occasion, John had come home to find the couple exchanging equally attentive acts of intimacy in the car while parked in our driveway waiting for Brooke. He explained to Brooke, that her choice to now be with a man did not erase the decisions she had made to be in a relationship with someone of the same sex and that, by definition, bi-sexuality did not make her any less of a lesbian. She still made a choice and acted on that decision. He explained that she could not negate the fact without also being a lesbian or bi-sexual.

Later, John related the same principal to his drug use before he met me. He explained that he made a choice to use drugs to excess. He admitted he was hooked, but knew that his choice to use drugs made him codependent and that would never change. He made the choice every day not to use again, when I told him that I would leave and never look back if he did. He said that didn't make him any less of an addict.

"Sometimes, when my mom is harping on me about my past mistakes," he explained, "I think she wants me to go back and change the history. What she doesn't understand, and never will, is that it is my history that made me who I am. Just like her history has made her who she is." He went on to say that some people concentrate on the mistakes of others because it takes their attention away from the things that make them feel like they have failed in their own life. "We all tell the story that makes us look better than the truth does. We never allow ourselves to see the blessings in making those poor decisions."

Shortly after John's death, Bill said something similar to this. He said, "There are three sides to every story. There is your side, my side, and the truth, which is usually somewhere in the middle. "

It wasn't until that day that I started to look for the blessings that came out of two events and recognizing that there were blessings that came from John's death. The ripple of those blessings would expand over the following years.

Chapter 16

Kindred Spirits

As the anniversary of John's death approached, I became more emotional and aware of the fact that John was never coming through that front door. Brooke and I agreed that there were nights when we still expected the door to open and him to be standing there, home from his witness protection. It was strange to admit that I knew that I was starting to realize this wasn't a dream and that I needed to allow myself to let go and have the cry I'd been denying myself for months. Even the counselor I was seeing every two weeks would ask me, "Have you allowed yourself to cry?"

Every time she asked me the question, I had to think what "allowing myself to cry" looked like. It was not that I had not shed any tears for John, as I had. In March, I finally decided to get some clarification from her. So, when the question came up in one of my last sessions, I answered the question with something more than denial. "What does that actually mean?" I asked her, looking her straight in the eye. "Are you asking me if I have wailed and beat my chest crying out in anguished racked sobs? Or, are you asking me if I recognize the sadness?"

The counselor stared back at me, as if she was waiting for me to say more. She remained silent without response. She just waited.

I decided to go on, "Do you mean have I shed copious amounts of tears, making myself incapable of coherent sentences? Or, are you asking if I cried for the loss of him?" Not waiting for her to respond, as I could tell she wasn't going to, I went on. "I've cried tears. I have felt guilt over his death, feeling like it should have been me. I have gotten angry. I have listened to everyone talk about how much they miss him, when they didn't have time for him while he was here. Are you asking if I have cried because of loneliness? Because I have had a few tears of loneliness. Or, are you asking me if I became a massive puddle because I found one of his damn chew tins under the bed?"

"All of it," she said. "I've been seeing you for ten months and you have never talked about any of that. In fact, I wondered why you were coming, as you were not crying here either. I didn't even know you were angry."

"To be honest, I have cried. But, I have not gone hysterical. And, loneliness is a state of mind because we are never alone. I don't cry with other people because this is the one thing that solely belongs to me. I don't have to share my grief with anyone. I don't have to listen to anyone telling me that they understand, or that death is easier than divorce-"

"Excuse me?" she interrupted me.

"Yeah, I was told by someone that it is easier to deal with death than divorce."

"How did you respond to that?"

"I didn't. But, if it is said to me again, I am going to pull out the tackle box with John's ashes, set it on the table and tell the person to reconcile with that! Divorce is a choice. I had no choice here."

My counselor kind of smiled at me, as I know she had heard enough from me to know that I would do that. "Has this person experienced both?"

"No, just divorce. But, I suspect the statement is more about his inability to let go of that experience than it is knowledge that death is easier. A corpse cannot argue, a spouse makes the decision to end the argument by walking away." There it was again! Making a decision to let go or hang on, trying to figure out what one could have done differently. It's over. Move on!

"You are correct that you are not alone. You have people that care about you and share this experience. You just need to reach out to them," she said.

I needed to tell her that wasn't what I meant. Maybe it was residual fear that I really was crazy, or just a need to see her reaction? Regardless, I was compelled to just be straight with her and see what happened next. "I am not talking about my support system! The reason why I have not just cried is because I am never alone. Whether you call them spirits, ghosts, souls, angels, they are all right there!"

"Well of course, your loved ones will always be in your heart," she stated.

"No, you don't get it!" I said. "I see them. They are all over the place. They are constantly with you."

"What are you talking about?"

"Angels," I sighed. "I see them. I feel them. I hear them. They are real."

"You see angels?" she asked, looking skeptical.

"Yes."

"What do they look like?"

I could tell she found this interesting, as she wasn't really writing anything down. In the beginning of our sessions, she made notes and wrote on a pad. On occasion, she would refer back to her notes. She wasn't writing. I had her full attention. "They look like bright lights, mostly."

"Do they have wings?" she asked me.

"Sometimes."

"What else are you seeing?"

"John. But, I smell his scent, too. You know what I mean?"

"Yes. How does he appear to you?"

"Usually in a white t-shirt, blue jeans and work boots."

"Is this real to you?"

"As real as you are."

For some reason, I cannot remember her name, the counselor that I was seeing for a year to help me deal with my grieving. However, I remember feeling comfortable with her. When she started writing on her notepad, I imagined words like "delusional" going into her notes. So, I proceeded to tell her about my most notable visits from spirit, including Heinrich. I abbreviated some of the story, in the interest of my paid amount of time. She took a few notes, but her expression changed with the stories.

When I had completed my tales of the past year, she put down her pad and pen and said, "Do you know what a medium is?"

"Yes," I said, "I am a medium."

"How long have you been a medium?" she asked me.

"I believe my whole life."

"I believe you," she said. "I am glad you have others that are helping you fine tune your gifts."

I felt an enormous amount of relief. Here was a person that could probably diagnose crazy pretty quickly. She was not making any phone calls to psychiatric wards to find me a spot. She just told me she believed me. I told her, "I think it was my head injury that allowed me to handle John's death," I told her. "Plus, his death reconnected me with my gift of sight."

"I think you are correct," she nodded her agreement. "Do you think that seeing spirit allows you to be comfortable with the passing?"

"I believe that is part of it. I mean," I tried to explain, "I feel the sadness and the heartache, but I know it's just part of my life. I see that death is also life for our spirit."

I needed to hear this from someone that didn't know this about me. Although she knew the history of my last year, I had never told her about angels. I reserved those discussions for my friends. She knew about how I was feeling about the death of my husband and my relations with family and friends in regards to that death. She also knew about some of my work issues, as I admitted to her, repeatedly, how much I hated being on the phone. But, she was the first person outside my circle of friends that I had told about my gifts. She didn't think I was crazy. She believed me. On my way home from that appointment, I allowed myself to cry. In fact, I did it so well that I had to pull over until I could see.

Most days, I talked on the phone, or listened to the radio, while driving home from my full-time job in Woodbury. Prior to her tonsillectomy in February, Cally was often sick. On those occasions, I would talk to Cally and try to find out how she was feeling. The company that we worked for had a pretty strict attendance policy and Cally, as well as myself, had walked the line of termination review on more than one occasion. Working in a call center required an individual to be at their desk, ready to take incoming calls for job security.

Shortly after John died, I was moved into a position to monitor phone calls for quality control. Occasionally, I would retrieve calls from the attendance line when our administrative guru was out on vacation. I walked a fine line with Cally at work, as she was one of my best friends outside of work. When I was doing attendance, it was hard to send write-up requirements to her supervisor. It was rare that I monitored her calls, but on occasion I did. Her phone voice was as beautifully sweet as she, so that never presented issues for me.

On my way home from work one day, I called her at home. When she answered, I could tell she was not well. "Hey! Are you all right?"

"Yes, I had to go to that surgery consult today," she reminded me. "I was in this morning."

"I know. I just didn't remember the consult."

We talked a little about what was going on during the day, when Cally asked me, out of nowhere, "When did I tell you about Caron?"

"What?" Cally and I had not talked about the night in the bar. I never talked to her about seeing Caron, or my conversation with her all the way home. There was no sense in me denying that she said something about her, but I wanted to make sure we were talking about the same Caron. Unfortunately, the only thing that came out of my mouth was, "what?"

"Don't play dumb with me!" she accused lightly, laughing. "I asked you if I told you about Caron?"

"You're angel, Caron?" I asked.

"Yes. That one."

"The night of your birthday party, when you were falling down, coming out of the bathroom without your pants pulled up, drunk," I said with a little irritation.

"I was not falling down without my pants drunk!"

"Ah, yeah, you were!" I relayed the story to her, telling her about the drive home from her party also.

"Shit! Nobody told me all that!"

"I thought your sister would've told you?" I asked, surprised.

There was a bit of a pause and then, she said, "What did my dad say?"

"Nothing. He just rolled his eyes and went back to playing pool with Andy." This is often how conversations with Cally went. We would get sidetracked from the initial question. "So, how did you know that you told me about Caron?"

"Oh yeah!" remembering her initial question herself. "She told me I should listen to you and have my liver checked. And, I told her that I just had all my blood draws for my surgery. She said, 'Toni knows about me and you both know about your liver.' What the hell? Why didn't you tell me you know about her?"

"Cally, I know about her. I have been seeing a lot of things. Hearing a lot of things. We haven't had time to talk. And, Brooke chose to leave again." This time, Brooke actually chose to leave and live with a friend's parents. She didn't want to live by my rules, again.

"Seeing a lot of things?"

"Angels, dead people, spirits, you name it."

"I KNEW IT! Why didn't you tell me?"

The moment of truth was upon me. I had to tell her how intimidated I was by her gifts. She gave one of the best massages around, could see and feel spirit like I could, and seemed to understand Brooke better than I. My self-confidence was zero on a scale of one to ten when it came to my own gifts and I was feeling like a failure with Brooke. I loved Cally. In that moment, I didn't want to tell her because I didn't want her to show me how she did it better. Was that envy? Jealousy? Fear? Probably all of them? Yet, there was also anger. I was angry with her for not taking care of her own health and for something she had no control over, her understanding of Brooke. I told her all of this and had to pull over again, because I was crying and she was yelling.

"Toni! I'm trying to help you with Brooke! The two of you are too much alike. John was your grounding post and now your energy is just bouncing off of each other! And, how dare you compare yourself to anyone- especially me! You give an awesome massage! In fact," she went on in her heated way, "I've had some of the best massages I've ever had from you in the past three months!"

"I wasn't fishing for a compliment. I am just telling you the truth. I am trying to figure all this out on my own."

"You don't have to do that! I'm really pissed off at you right now!"

"Ok? I am just being honest. And, you can be angry with me if you want, but I'm angry too. I'm angry that you have not had your liver checked. Now, you are looking at another procedure because your stomach sticks out and you haven't gotten your liver checked? What the hell, Cally?"

"Furthermore," she broke in, "I am a step-child and I understand how Brooke feels. Though, my biological father was just a sperm donor and my step-dad is and will always be my dad. John was a good father and he loved you and Brooke. And, Brooke is being a normal teenager. I'm not criticizing what you have done. I think you were right to kick her out. If I ever disrespected my dad the way she does you, I would have gotten worse! She's lucky to have you and she doesn't get it."

"And, you just avoided the topic of getting your liver checked."

"I've been to 5 clinics in Wisconsin and someone would have mentioned it by now. I don't know if I can even talk to you anymore tonight."

"Why the hell not?!"

"Because I am mad!"

"So, get over it!" I said. We sounded like cats fighting from opposite sides of a tall fence.   Neither one of us could get to the other because we were trapped on opposite sides. "I'm sorry if I made you mad. I am just working through this."

"Get over it, huh? That sounds like John."

"Yep."

"I miss Cheetos too, you know." Cally referred to John as Cheetos because of a stand-up comedian named Ron White. John used one of his lines every time he answered the phone when Cally called. She would ask him what he was doing and he would tell her he was sitting naked on a bean bag, eating Cheetos.

"I know. This sucks."

"I want you to talk to me about what is going on and let me help you."

"Well, you knew about all the sound stuff and the lights. I just didn't figure it out until Heinrich. Just don't be mad. I love you and need someone to hang out with on Friday nights."

"I need a massage. Want to do a trade?"

"Yes. But, not back-to-back I want mine on a different day."

As quickly as it started, our heated argument was over and we were making plans for a movie night. There are a few of my friends that I don't get together with if I cannot plan to spend hours with them. Cally and I would spend time together, planning on dinner and a movie, only to still be chatting at 3 in the morning. Tara and I would meet for coffee and 5 hours later, still be talking. Time would just slip away while we were discussing whatever topics we needed to address. Yet, it always felt like I had just arrived and we had just started talking.

As I pulled into my driveway, I told Cally I needed to go in and change clothes to go work at the chiropractic office. We made plans to do a trade of massage, me coming to her place one day and her coming to mine on Thursday. Of course, I knew that she would ask all sorts of questions at work the next day.

In late 2009, I started painting again. I had taken a watercolor class through community education a few years earlier. But, my habit of staying up until all hours of the night painting irritated John enough that I put it away. I took it out again because I could leave it out on my kitchen table now, not having to worry about anyone bitching at me for not eating, or sleeping. Painting was one of the few things that put me totally at peace. Plus, watercolor was forgiving. I loved the 'accidents' that happened when the water moved somewhere I did not want it to go. I connected so well with my own spirit while painting that I could work with the imperfections. It became one of my healing necessities. I started putting aside time for creating my art.

Out of my painting that fall came a healing piece so peaceful to me that I framed it and put it in my treatment space in March. The image I created was of a canoe on the sandy shore of a moonlit lake. It was the piece that helped me out of my funk in late October. When I framed it and put it onto my wall, I noticed the angels in that piece. They were hidden in the trees, watching me. I realized that this was symbolic of my intuitive awakening. The angels were always there, I just chose not to see them.

When Cally came in for her massage, she saw the painting on the wall and commented how it was so peaceful. She told me that it was perfectly me. It was that session with her where I actually saw some of the stuff she was dealing with on her daily intuitive path. She had told me that she felt like she was always being watched and that the beings that were watching her were not all together safe. She was correct, as the things that I saw watching her while I massaged did not feel heaven-sent. Though her angels confirmed my concern, they told me to allow them to deal with the lower level energies attached to her. I told Cally about them and what I was seeing. I also told her that her angels were going to take care of them.

I was getting close to the end of her massage when I was telling her about everything that I was seeing. The only reason why I shared anything at all was because she was asking me to share my experience with her. When I explained that I felt she had "watchers," she said that she knew about them, as they come at her in her sleep. Her cat would wake her up hissing and batting at things that were not necessarily visible to most people. Cally could see them. I could see them. Apparently, her cat, Nala, could see them, too.

I was working on her left arm and hand, when Cally said to me, "Toni, I think I am done."

Not understanding what she was saying, I asked, "Oh? Do you want me to quit massaging?" We were almost done, so I did not understand why she was saying this.

"No," she laughed. "I feel like I have done what I am supposed to do on this earth."

I don't know if I had a look of horror on my face or not, but the thought of her being done gave me a sinking feeling in the pit of my stomach. "What are you saying?" I whispered it. I could not get my voice any louder.

She looked at me and the energy in the room had changed completely. Everything went completely still. "I'm not going to off myself!" she explained. "I just get this feeling like I am done here?"

At the time, I felt the angels affirming what she was saying and did not want to even acknowledge it. I couldn't even think of losing her. She was like a sister. I talked to her every day. What would I do without her? These were all questions that went through my mind. Then, the softness of a feather touched my cheek. When and if this Earth angel did pass, I knew that I would be able to connect with her again. The angel by my side was communicating with me without words, bringing calmness to the idea that I would be losing my friend.

"I worry about my mom, Jenny and Mattie," she confessed.

"Why?" I asked. "They all have Terry. He's a rock. And, Jenny has Andy."

"Because I know my mom has experienced some of the same things in her life that I have. And, I have to admit, we all use alcohol to self-medicate."

"Well, I trust that they will be fine. So, will you, Cal."

"The weird thing is that I know that.   I don't want to die yet, but I know I've done this before."

"What? You've died before?"

"Yes."

Although I could feel the correctness of her answer, I had to ask her, "How do you know?"

"I had this dream last week, but it was more like a memory. I saw myself as a mom, with a little girl running around the kitchen."

"Did the yard have wildflowers and a wooden fence?"

"Yes?"

"I had the same dream about you." I said it, not because I remembered having the dream, but because I saw pictures of the dream in front of me, right there in the massage room. But, that was crazy! Was it not? I described the imagery that I was seeing. But, it was like I was in the scene too.

"That was exactly it!" She was excited about it and looked at me. "You were there too! Toni, you're my earth angel!"

"What? Shut up!"

"No really! That is how I see you! I know I will see you again."

"Well, thank you, but I don't know if I am or not. I think I am just gifted with the ability to discern angels."

"You have so many with you all the time, it makes sense."

For some reason, I could not agree with that comment. How could I be an angel on Earth? If I looked back at my life, I was not the most angelic person. At least, I could not remember a time when I wasn't a pain in someone's ass. There were still things that I could not remember about my past, but I'm sure that virtuous living was not my forte, then or now. I made some sarcastic remarks and we both laughed a bit. We didn't talk about her being "done" again.

Chapter 17

Full Circle

Brooke moved out of the apartment around the middle of March. She packed her clothes and some of her things, leaving still a majority of her belongings, stating she would be coming back for them. I asked her if she wanted to go to mass with my Mom and me on the anniversary of her father's death and she told me she would think about it. One of the things she took with her was a stand-alone punching bag that John and I gave her for Christmas the year before he died. She had asked for it. On several occasions after John died, I caught her punching and kicking it. One time, she even had tears in her eyes while doing it.

This was the first time she was leaving without me pushing her out the door. The funny thing was that she stated she was leaving because she didn't like my rules. At the same time, she needed that structure. Her anxiety was her worst enemy. She wanted to be on medication for it, but didn't want to go to counseling. Because of the addiction issues in her family, I explained that there may be healthier ways to deal with depression and anxiety. I told her that "covering up the pain with medication did not make it go away." Several of her family members were on various medications for anxiety and depression, but they were not doing anything else to overcome the issue. I believed that our western medicine model was sorely lacking in ethics when it came to the mental health of our society. Sure, the drugs cover up the pain and make you feel better, until you come off them. Having a co-dependent relationship with an anti-anxiety medicine is the same as any other addiction. John's addition to crack was no different than another's addition to Zoloft. Eventually, the body will present that mental pain in a physical way. We get another pill for that condition and then another pill.

At the time, I was aware that chemical reactions in the brain cause anxiety and depression. In my own counseling, I was told that I could be prescribed an anti-depressant by a doctor. There were many people telling me to see my doctor and have her prescribe something to "help me through" my grief. This idea that a pill was going to fix my anxiety and depression over the death of my husband pissed me off. If I really wanted to cover up the pain, I would have gone in the bottle with the other drunks! Plus, that pill was not going to remove the issue and bring my husband back. So, why would I prolong my agony by not working through the pain? What people fail to realize is the chemical reaction that the doctor was medicating them for just became more compounded by another chemical. I wasn't about to do that to myself and I sure as hell was not going to tell my daughter that it was okay for her to do it!

What I did say to her, was the same thing I have said to every person I have ever talked to about this topic. I told her that if she was going to take a pill for her anxiety, she needed to continue going to a psychologist to work through the things that are causing her anxiety. However, there are many people who are put on these drugs who stop getting counseling. They stop talking about the things that created that chemical reaction causing them to be depressed or anxious. Even if they don't know why they are depressed, they should be talking to a trained professional and not just taking a medication to adjust the chemical in their brain. The body, by design, naturally does emit chemicals to ward off a threat to the homeostatic condition. The body will continue to adjust to those emotional and physical wounds we are experiencing. I believe that the many chemicals in our food, water, living and working environments are responsible for the decline of our mental and physical health.

"Every counselor I have seen told me I needed to be on drugs," Brooke claimed.

"You've only seen one counselor, Brooke. And, if she told you that, I'm pretty sure she didn't say that you should be on drugs and that there was nothing else that she could do for you. It only covers up the pain. It doesn't take it away. When you are off the drug, the pain comes back."

Brooke's response was, "I would rather cover up the pain than feel this."

"So, you cover up the pain for the rest of your life and never deal with the root cause, which has nothing to do with Dad's death." Although she seemed angry when she left, she didn't seem to disagree.

The week before the anniversary, I took some time off. I was sick for most of that time. To be honest, I think this was how my grief was manifesting in my body. I would eat something and vomit within 10 minutes of eating. I didn't have a fever, but I did not want to get out of bed. So, I happened to be home when my auto insurance company called and left a message. I still was not answering the phone, unless it was someone I knew. So, I called the claims adjuster, Charlotte, back within an hour of the call.

One of the things that I was grateful for in all of this was the fact that John was the only fatality in the accident. The only other person that was sustainably injured was the man in the Volkswagen Golf that stopped John's forward motion down the highway. The man was flown by helicopter to a Twin Cities hospital where he underwent several surgeries for a broken femur. There was one other girl treated at Baldwin Medical Center for cuts and abrasions. She was one of two passengers in the car that was sideswiped. Other than the accident report, I never saw anything else regarding injuries. In fact, there was documentation that the other two individuals in the sideswiped vehicle had refused medical attention. Yet, here was Charlotte, calling to tell me that the second passenger in the sideswiped car was suing for medical damages.

"What?" I asked the claims adjuster in disbelief.

"One of the passengers in the car is suing for damages. I am calling you to let you know that if she is awarded damages above the limits of the policy, you will be responsible for those charges."

Working in the insurance world for 10 years had its advantages. I understood what she was saying, but did not understand how I would be getting this now, after almost a year. The woman in question had a Biblical name and was related to the driver somehow. And, when the adjuster told me that the individual just filed the suit, I could not stop myself from saying, "She should be suing her parents for that name!"

Charlotte was professional enough not to laugh at my smart-ass comment. She explained the limitations of my policy and told me that their legal department will handle the case on their end. "The only time you need to be involved is if the case goes before a judge and the judge finds in her favor."

Further, she explained that I would get a copy of the legal claim and the lawyer's deposing documents at a later date. Charlotte answered my questions about the claims processing and explained the resolution with the other claimants in the accident.

When I hung up the phone, I did not feel sick anymore. I felt angry. Some ambulance chaser would not let me put this in my past. I would have to deal with it for at least another ninety days. "What a crock of shit!" I hissed to the wall of my apartment. "What could she have possibly lost that is worth that lawsuit?" On the new steam, I showered and got out of the house with the angels assuring me everything would be fine.

On Saturday, March 27, 2010, I went to Cally's for a massage. When I got there, her neighbor was having an "everything must go" sale in her condominium. We decided to go in and check out what she had for sale. Aside from furniture and household items, she had books and bins full of crafting items. I grabbed it, deciding to buy the bin full of craft items. Then, I found two books that seemed to call me. I was looking at one of them and the neighbor said, while pointing to the book in my other hand, "I think this one was meant for you to have."

"Why do you think that?" I asked. It wasn't that I didn't believe in other people's intuition, but I had never met this person, so I was cautious.

"I don't know. I'm kind of intuitive that way," she explained.

Both of the books were about financial matters and money management. The one she pointed out read more towards the energetics of creating a successful business. So, I decided to buy the craft bin and the book she pointed out. I was always looking for things to read these days. Reading was quiet and required my concentration. I was never a strong reader, as it felt slow and cumbersome to me. However, I loved to read things that interested me because it took me to a different place. I needed the mental rest.

My mom told me once that I was like my dad when I read something interesting to me. "The house could explode and your father wouldn't know because his nose was in a book." During my marriage, there were many nights that the lamp on my nightstand would burn well past midnight until John made me just close the book where I was. He thought it was nonsense that I had to finish the chapter. Typically, his action was so that he could actually go to sleep. He, too, was an avid reader. It would frustrate me when I would come to bed with the intention of reading a chapter or two and upon my settling in my position next to him on the bed, he would close the book that he'd been reading for five minutes and lay down.

"So, what are you girls doing today?" the neighbor asked.

"I am getting a massage because today is a tough anniversary." The woman asked a question and I explained that my husband had been killed a year before in a car accident. As I said this, the woman's face and demeanor changed completely. She expressed her condolences, but there was something about her energy that completely changed.

When Cally and I got back into her place, Cally said, "Did you notice how her whole attitude shifted? It was like she couldn't get us out of there fast enough?"

"Yeah! She kind of turned gray," I confirmed.

Cally gave me a massage, and by the time we were done, we were running late. We still had to get to my Mom's house and meet Brooke. We were going to the evening mass. Yet, John came in during my massage. "John's here," she told me as she worked on my neck. While she worked, she relayed what was happening. As she worked, she noticed a green crystal above my heart and angels circling the table. There were so many in the room, that Cally said she felt crowded. But, she also felt the love they had for me.

I could feel John holding my left hand. He was having conversation with Cally, but I could not hear the words. As I lay there, Cally continued to work and describe what he was saying. She said, "He wants you to know that he has to go away for a while, but that he loves you and will come back when he is finished with his schooling."

"Oh, he's not going fishing this time?" I said sarcastically. I heard a chorus of laughter, as if there were thirty people in the room. Cally was talking into my right ear, while John was laughing in my left.

"Something important is happening," Cally whispered it urgently. "The angels just parted to make a path."

"Archangel Michael is here," I said, without opening my eyes. His bold presents grounded me, making me feel strong. I knew that Michael's presence was very important. He was one of the angels that I saw all the time in the beginning of my intuitive awakening. I would call him in to protect me.

"John's got to go now." Her voice was full of awe as she described that Michael had knighted John with his sword and tapped the top of our enfolded hands. She stopped talking, suddenly, because she couldn't talk. Her tears were dripping on my face. As I felt John kiss me on my cheek, I could feel her tear run down into mine. I could feel myself letting go of any need to have him here, knowing that he would always be there when I needed him. I heard him whisper that he loved me and he was gone.

"He left with Michael," my friend explained, weeping openly. "That was powerful and important."

"The Sword of Michael," I whispered.

"What?"

"Cally, John is the Sword of Michael."

"He knighted John and blessed you. He tapped your hands with his sword."

"I know. I felt it. But, John is the Sword of Michael."

Cally went to church with me after my massage. Then, we went to dinner with my Mom, Brooke and her current boyfriend, and a friend who had served communion at my wedding, named Rosemary. I didn't tell Brooke about the visit from John until much later. That experience was for Cally and I to share. We were both still talking about it when we got back to Cally's home around 10 p.m. We talked for another three hours until I realized how exhausted I was. When I finally got home from River Falls, it was 2:00 a.m.

In the next few weeks, I did not see John's spirit at all. Easter was in early April and I was spending it at my Mom's. Yet, Cally talked me into a facial. We found a young woman in Hudson that was doing facials out of her parents' home. Again, we met up and went for our facials together. It was a great experience and I knew this girl was going places, which she did. In six years, she has built her own beauty empire with her own make-up line and stores in the Twin Cities and around the country.

After our facials, we went shopping at Maurice's, with Cally bringing piles of clothes in and out of my dressing room. I did buy a couple shirts, but could not find any pants that fit me comfortably. I was getting overwhelmed by all of it, as it wasn't often that I actually bought clothes for myself. Actually, I hated shopping. My personal feelings about my body were not positive and when faced with my reflection in a three way mirror, it became hellish. I was not comfortable. Plus, both of us needed to go to our respective parents' houses and we were late. I had to go home, feed my cat and then drive back through Hudson.

The next day, I went to Easter Mass with Mom. Since my accident, churches were over-stimulating. Not only could I feel the energy of everyone in the room, but I could see their angels. It took me a long time to understand that I did not have to channel all of it. This was due, in part, to the fact that I did not even realize that I was channeling these energies. Also, I was so interested in learning how to deal with my gifts that I was trying to learn how to work with them when angels were present. Anytime there were crowds, there were also angels.

While sitting in the pew next to my mother, I tried to just concentrate on what the priest was saying. However, my mind kept wandering off. I caught myself thinking that I had turned into a 'C&E.' This was the term that parishioners used for people that only came to mass on Christmas and Easter. John and I had tried to go to a couple churches around New Richmond, but did not find one that felt comfortable. As I sat there in Easter Mass, I realized that church did not have the same pull for me. I did not have to belong to a church because I did not need other people to validate my faith. The Catholics believe that parishioners are there to bear witness for each other in their faith journey. But, my faith was strong. I did not have the same idea of God that I did before my traumatic brain injury. Yet, I knew that we have a source energy that serves our highest good. Church was just ritual. Plus, I realized that I did not need to have my butt in the seat to know that I was connected to every person in the church. I knew that I was connected to everything in the Universe.

"Where do you find God?" I heard Father ask in his homily.

"Not here," I thought. I hope I didn't say it aloud, as I could have. That was the other thing I noticed about my gifts. On occasion, information comes right through my brain and out of my mouth without my conscious knowledge that I am spewing information. I imagine that if I had said it out loud, my mother would have given me "the look".

There was movement around me in the ethereal world. Some of the things I saw that day in church, I did not understand. For example, there were things there that seemed evil to me. I wondered how these things could be in a place that was protected by God, or Divine power. I must have posed the question, as an answering voice drifted in telling me that it was not the time or place to be discussing it. Then, I was told that I was protected, so no harm would come to 'any part of me.'

Instantly, I understood that 'any part of me' referred to everyone in the church. It was just a knowing. The angels did not have to clarify that, I just knew. If I am connected to God, Source, or the Universe, than I am connected to everyone in the church. They are a part of me, as I am a part of them. I hadn't even had communion, and yet, I was transformed.

When we were walking out of church, I realized I had gotten through the mass without hearing anything after the Gospel reading. I didn't cry, as I did on the anniversary. I didn't start to giggle, thinking of Kramer from an episode of *Seinfeld*. And, I didn't hear more than half of mass. I remember the entrance music and singing along. I did not remember, however, the blessing of the gifts, the readings, the Lord's Prayer, or any of the other rituals that make up Mass. If someone had asked me, they may have thought I was sleeping. I could tell you who the priest was, as there was only one in the church. But, I could not tell you how he related the story of the Bible to current life, or if he even did.

Chapter 18

Another Beginning

The week after Easter, I bought a new washer and dryer for my apartment. The ones we had bought second hand seven years earlier were leaking out the bottom onto the floor. The technology available allowed for sanitizing and steam cleaning in the washer and dryer. As a massage therapist, that was important to me because I washed my sheets at home. In addition to the sanitization option, the loads used less water and soap.

The next big thing that happened was the conclusion of my grief counseling on Tuesday after work. Through mutual agreement, my counselor and I determined that I was handling my grief normally. She did say that I was welcome to come back at any time I felt I needed. For some reason, I think that I had met the limitations of my insurance benefits for my mental health. Again, the not-so-shocking reality of a health care system driven by government policy and insurance monopolies made me glad that I was not mentally incapacitated from my brain injury.

As I left work on Wednesday, I was feeling like there was something I was missing. I had an easier evening, as my schedule was open after my one client at the clinic, so I was free to relax. I was on my cell phone, speaking to Bill, at a stop light. The light changed and I started to roll forward to accelerate. I dumped the clutch and killed the Jeep. I had just gotten it started again and was about to accelerate when I was rear-ended. Everything on my dashboard and front seat flew past me into the back of the Wrangler. My phone flew backwards as my head snapped forward and slammed back into the head rest of my driver's seat. Unbelieving, I looked into the review mirror to see a burnt orange Avalanche with a smashed in front grill. The woman driving was looking down at her lap as I reached for the door lever.

After speaking with the woman for a second, I wanted to get out of the intersection and allow traffic through. So, I drove across the four lanes straight into the entrance of a parking lot for a huge building that was once the corporate headquarters for State Farm Insurance. I got out of the car, my neck and shoulders already screaming, and looked at the back of my Wrangler. The angels were telling me to move slowly, the whole time I was asking, "Why now?"

"Are you all right?" the driver from the other vehicle asked me.

So many people, after similar accidents, deny any injury at the scene of the accident because they do not feel the effects immediately, only to find out days, months and years later that there were unreported injuries that surfaced later. Having worked with accident injuries in my massage practice with the chiropractor, I knew that I had 72 hours to feel worse than I did at that moment. Knowing this, I answered, "I don't know."

"Do you need an ambulance?" the girl asked.

"No, I need the police. My phone flew off my dashboard into the back seat somewhere."

The whole time she was speaking with me, the woman was looking down at her phone texting someone. Then, she called 911. Although I did not tell the police when they arrived, I suspected the woman had been texting when she plowed into me. I refused the offer of an ambulance with the police officer and the woman from the Avalanche. I was not going into a hospital. I would go to my chiropractor before I went to the doctor.

My little Wrangler had become affectionately known to me and John as "Toni's Tank." In the 10 years of owning the vehicle, I had hit two deer, a turkey, was in a front-end collision that caused a chain reaction of bumper hitting bumper. Not to mention, I went through a three month period of hitting over 8 birds when they flew into my window. Plus, a horse ran into me. None of these things caused any body damage. Until that Avalanche pushed my rear spare tire into the half door and folded it in, I thought the little vehicle was indestructible.

I remember telling my old chiropractor that the Wrangler was the only vehicle with a roll bar. To which he said, "And, you are the only person I know that needs one." We laughed because it was possibly true. I was kind of graceless.

Yes, I had a dented back door. Yet, out of the two vehicles, the Avalanche sustained 10 times more damage. I looked at her truck, which appeared to be fairly new, and realized that she had to have launched into me. We both had been at a full stop, waiting for the left hand turn light to give us an arrow. While I could drive my Jeep home, she wasn't going to be driving her vehicle far with the radiator leaking and front grill dragging. I felt pretty lucky.

The next day, I was leaving work early to take delivery of my washer and dryer. I forced myself to work, but had such a headache and neck ache, that I called my massage appointments and cancelled them. I did get adjusted by Doctor Leo. I also talked to Cally about getting a massage, because I knew that I would need some work.

"You should go out with Wendy and me tomorrow night," Cally said.

"I'll have to see how I feel."

"I can give you a massage before we go out?"

"Let's plan on that."

The next day, I called into work. I could not even stand, let alone drive. I had dizziness again, as I did from my head injury. Plus, the spirits in the apartment were moving around and whispering again. I couldn't figure out what was going on. Yet, I knew I was not getting a massage. I called and let Cally know that I would not be going out with her and Wendy, nor getting a massage.

When I got home after the accident on Wednesday night, I found the court documents in my mailbox from the lawyer the insurance company had assigned to the case regarding John's accident. I read through the document and found out that the woman was not only naming my insurance company, but the companies for the other two drivers involved and Eau Claire Medical Group. I read it to make sure that the assigned lawyer pointed out the refusal for medical treatment at the scene of the accident, which it did have.

As I was home, I decided to start reading the book that I had bought from Cally's neighbor on the anniversary. I realized within ten minutes why the woman had turned that greyish color and her behavior had changed. The woman writing the story was explaining how she had to figure out how to make money because her husband and child were killed in a car accident. The book discussed the Law of Attraction and how small ideas become huge sources of income when we trust our higher power. Although, I am sure Cally's neighbor was mortified after recommending the book to me and then finding out that my husband had died in a car accident, she gifted me with something that made sense to me.

This led me to think about the blessings that come from those things in my life that I believed, at the time, were going to destroy me. For example, I really did not know that I would still be with my employer after my head injury. There were days when I felt that they would fire me because I could not remember my job. I had individuals who pointed me to resources, but I had to relearn the knowledge that put me in my position in the first place. My head injury showed me my strength and resilience, rather than just my weaknesses. Then, I was convinced that my head injury allowed me to handle John's death in a free flowing manner. While the injury brought me back to my gifts, the death of John showed me how I would use them. I would not be working with my gifts if it had not been for John showing up in the car. I could not have one without the other.

I was further blessed that I was unable to have children. If I had a child, I would be raising it by myself. It was hard enough dealing with a teenager who had lost her only confidante. How would I have dealt with a younger child under 10?

Over the year, I realized I had become one again, without my spouse. When we married, we became each other's other half. Upon death, I had split in two. In many ways, I felt that my soul had split in half as much as my heart had. One half picked up the responsibility of doing what I had contracted for in the beginning of this lifetime, while the other half died with John. Or, maybe it had split when I fell and that half waited for John to go? When I asked my Divine guidance, they indicated that it did split in half so that I could expand and stand as one, without John. They did caution that John had to make the choice to go in that accident, too.

There were many other blessings. I did not have to make a decision to take John off of life support. I did not have to watch him live a life he would have hated- being incapable of hunting and fishing, talking or walking. I was blessed that he made the choice to go, sparing me the worry of taking care of him. In my reflecting, I knew there would be many blessings for years to come from both my head injury and the death of my spouse. These blessings I would not have had without the events that occurred.

Over the weekend, I spent time counting the blessings I had while icing my neck. I took time for journaling and reading. I watched movies and had popcorn. For the first time in over a year, the angels and most of the spirits present let me rest. They allowed me to sleep until 10:00 on Saturday and Sunday morning. My body hurt, but I was rested.

On Monday, I was still having issues with dizziness and nausea from my neck, so I called into work. At this point, I didn't even care if they fired me for attendance. I could not go back to work and sit in a cramped cube for 8 hours taking calls. Although I did not have any misconception that I was not replaceable, I was one hundred percent sure that my supervisor did not know how to do half of what I did. So, if my supervisor did have to fire me for attendance, the evil part of me was kind of laughing at the prospect of her trying to step in until the company allowed her to spend money on another subject matter expert.

Cally called me late that night, while she was on her walk. She had to work at her part-time job in a home for adults with disabilities. She slept there some nights and got the residents ready in the morning for their jobs. "I can give you a massage tomorrow after work," she huffed into the phone.

"That works. I will be in tomorrow."

"You were missed today. There was a cluster bomb of crap!" She explained some of the day's work drama, making me even happier that I stayed home.

"Sorry I cancelled tonight again."

"It's fine. Wendy and I went tanning."

"Good."

"We bought packages. When you are feeling better, we should go get another facial."

"Sure."

"Hey, Tone, I have to go. My mamma is calling and I have to talk to her before I go to work."

"OK. See you tomorrow. Don't be late!"

"I won't. One more occurrence and I am done." Again, Cally was skimming the line of being fired at her full-time job. She didn't want that to happen because she was planning on having a sleeve put on her stomach for weight loss. She had already had the psychiatric evaluation, met with the doctor and started trying to lose some weight. She would need her full-time job for the insurance that would pay for it.

Shortly after we hung up, I got ready for bed. I had gotten in the habit of bringing my laptop to bed and playing games online until I was sleepy. For some reason, I decided to write in my journal before bed, turning off the light around 11:00 PM. If I was getting up at 6 for work, I needed to get some sleep.

At about 4:30 AM, I woke up to John's laughter and Cally's cheery voice asking, "Cheetos, what are you doing here?" Looking around in the darkness of the early morning light, I did not see John's spirit at all. And, of course, Cally wasn't there. For some reason, I wrote this in my journal and laid back down, falling back to sleep quickly.

Ninety minutes later, I was hitting the snooze on my alarm clock and pushing the cat off my chest. I had closed the journal and completely forgot about the dream when I got up ten minutes later. It wasn't until I was eating my breakfast that I realized that it was so quiet in the apartment. My angels were there, but they were not talking. They were just energetically supporting me. Yet, something felt wrong. I didn't know what it was, but it felt off. So, I asked Timothy, "What is going on?"

My guardian angel just looked back at me and shook his head. He was telling me something in another language. The language felt ancient, though I had no idea what the origin of it was. I did not understand what he was saying and asked him to repeat it. "You aren't ready yet. But, we are here when you are," he said.

"I'm not ready for what?"

"It is a truth that can only be spoken in our language."

"Should I understand that language?" I asked, perplexed.

"You do. But, that has not come back to you yet."

As I had to get on my way to work, I did not ask more questions. What kept drawing my attention was that gut feeling that something was shifting. There was a change surfacing from the depths of my knowledge that I knew was substantial. I knew that this was important to me and I was not going to like it. Something had happened and it tilted the energy in my world even further than it was already tilted. That dizziness from my accident the week before felt too much like the dizziness from my head injury. I felt turned upside down.

I pulled into the parking lot at work and Cally's red Neon was not parked in its usual spot. "Oh shit!" I thought. She started at the same time I did, but was there before me. The times when she was not early, it was usually her part-time job that slowed her down. She had to wait for her relief to get there before she could leave. If her car wasn't there, she was either late, or called in. Either way, she would be up for termination.

After getting in the building and dropping my stuff at my desk, I went over to Cally's desk. Wendy was there taking calls. I waited until she was between calls and said, "Have you heard from Cally this morning?"

"No," said Wendy. "The last time I talked to her was last night."

"Yeah," I said, "me too. I spoke with her on her walk." As Wendy's phone rang, I went back to my desk to log into my computer. I called into the attendance line to see if Cally had called in to say she was going to be late. There was no call from her. I called Cally's cell phone from my desk and it went to her voice mail. I took some supervisor calls and answered some questions, as all the supervisors were not available to be logged into the line.

In my new position, I sat with another quality control specialist who came in about thirty minutes after I did. We sat next to an internal wall with a tall, solid fabric covered wall. Unless you walked down the aisle, you could not see us from the walkway in the call center. The white noise that was piped into our area was constantly humming. When Kari came in, I was working on a monitor. As she and I had a lot in common, I considered her a friend. I told her that I was worried that Cally was going to lose her job because she wasn't there. On the other side of Kari's wall, our administrative person who does the attendance had just come into work and overheard me saying that Cally wasn't there. By 9:00 AM, I was very concerned about Cally.

When my cell phone rang at my desk at 9:30, I was on another supervisor call at my desk. I looked down and saw the name of the caller on my phone. It was Cally's Mom, Kathy. As soon as I was off the phone, I listened to the message left on my voice mail, put my work phone in an unavailable state and called Kathy back.

"Hello?" Kathy said.

"Kathy, this is Toni. I got your message to call you right away. What's going on?" Kari was sitting next to me.

"Cally's gone."

"What do you mean, Cally's gone?" I asked her.

"She's gone!" Kathy wailed into the phone. Immediately, I felt a hurt so deep and unfathomable, I didn't want her to have to explain. I knew. Yet, I had to let her say it.

"Kathy, can you tell me what has happened?"

The sobs tore through the phone. I could feel them and asked angels to go to her, without even realizing I was doing it. "The sheriff came and told me that she did not wake up this morning. She was found by her co-worker. She's dead! My beautiful girl is dead."

"She's dead? But, I just spoke with her last night!"

"I did too."

"Is Terry home?" I asked.

"No, he's on his way home. I thought I should call you, so you could let her supervisor know."

"Kathy, I am so sorry. I will handle everything here." Kari was there, looking at me in shock. She had heard me talking to her. I hung up with Kathy and looked at Kari. Moments ticked and I did not feel anything. Kari got up and hurried to get the administrator. I sat there alone, a single tear coming out my eye.

"Toni? I'll drive you home. You shouldn't be driving."

I looked up to see Dawn and Kari standing there. They were ready to get me out of there before I lost all composure. What they didn't realize was that I was not going to lose composure. I would grieve, but not at that moment. Everyone who knew her loved her and there were at least 30 people in that call center who needed to be told. I wanted to make sure that they were told. I would allow them to take me home, but first I had to be there for them. I said as much to Dawn and Kari.

All of a sudden, all the supervisors were out of their meetings. The Director of our department was organizing small groups of employees to be told, ushering them into a conference room. I don't even remember being there when they told Wendy. However, I know she took it very hard, as did I. All I could think of was, "Why her?"

"Because she was done," the answer came in from Caron, softly. She was not visibly present for me, but I felt her. And, in my head, I promised that I was going to have a talk with her later.

I stayed until my boss came over to my desk and told me that I needed to go home. I was told that Kari and Dawn would be taking me. They were not going to let me drive. I was fine, but my argument that I could get home on my own was not being received. I suppose, this was for my safety as well as that of others. They may have felt that I was in shock and just not showing emotion because of it. Regardless, I went home with Kari driving my manual transmission and Dawn following us.

Chapter 19

Fly Away

After Kari and Dawn had left, I changed into more casual attire, stuffed a sandwich in my face and called Cally's mom, telling her that I would be up there in a little while. As I walked out to go, Bill was coming home and stopped me. "Why are you home?" he asked.

I explained to him about Cally. He had met her, but did not know her that well. Regardless, he offered to go with me to her parents and asked me to wait. "You really should not be going up there alone."

"I am fine. Why do people not believe this?" I asked. Part of me wanted to have a friend along for the ride, while the other part of me wanted to talk to spirit on my trip. I needed to process this in my own way and my processing did not involve emotional release. Yes, Cally was gone and I was sad that I no longer had my companion, but her spirit was free. There was so much peace in understanding that fact. I had learned in the last year that death of a body did not mean death of the soul and spirit. The spirit lived on and the soul transcended to another level.

"I think you are in shock, Toni," Bill said quietly. "Your friend just died and you don't even seem upset. That is not normal."

"What is normal?" I asked. "I understand you are concerned about me, but I know that there are blessings in this, too." I knew he would understand this statement, as I had spoken to Bill about the blessings that come from loss. I understood that the concept appealed to his religious knowledge. He seemed to accept it and quit harping on the symptoms of shock. I wasn't about to tell him that I felt I already knew she was gone before I went to work.

When we got to Kathy and Terry's place, there were tables in the garage covered in food. There were people there already. I gave Kathy a hug and she began to sob, telling me the story of the sheriff coming to her home that morning. "She had died in her sleep. One of the staff went in to wake her when he got there at 6:00, as none of the residents were ready for work. He told the sheriff that she was already gone when he got there." I listened, feeling everything she was feeling, but not expressing it. I just absorbed it and sent it to her angels.

The sheriff deputy did not even stay with her until Terry got home. He told her what happened and was called away. I did not have to imagine the confusion Kathy felt, as I could feel it. How does a parent understand that their child

257

was mysteriously stolen by death in the middle of the night? How does a parent understand why it was their 36- year-old daughter's turn to go and that they, themselves, were not done yet? I am not aware of any parent who, having lost a child, has not said, "It should have been me," or "A parent is not supposed to survive their children."

Although I understood this was part of the grieving process, as I had also had these thoughts when I had miscarriages and when I lost John, I was beginning to awaken to the selfishness of those statements. What I was really saying when I made those comments as a grieving mother and wife was, "it should have been me because I don't want to feel this pain." What I failed to understand was that if it had been me, my husband, mother, friends and other family would have had to go through the same pain I was feeling. From where I was standing, the only person that would have been better for would have been the person saying it.

Then, I started to think about what spirit meant by being done. I had read that we all have a contract that we enter into before coming into this life. In fact, there were many psychics that said this before I started reading about it. I was a head injury away from drinking that glass of Kool Aid the first time I heard that. So, if our soul actually did have a contract to fulfill, it would be disrespectful of me to discredit the fact that someone had fulfilled their contract in this lifetime by saying, "it should have been me."

I wanted to tell Kathie about the blessings that would come. I wanted to explain to her that Cally was not gone forever. I wanted to be able to show her the joys that I saw for her. Grandchildren would bless her life. Her other children would bring her joyous things. She could not forget them in her grief, as they were grieving, too. I wanted to tell her, but the angels told me it was not her time to know these things. It was not for me to tell her. They told me to allow her to learn in her own way, her own time. This was her grief, not mine. I was there to witness and be supportive because I loved Cally. She was my sister. She was my earth angel. She was my Callifina, as I was her Tonifina.

It wasn't until I returned to my apartment that I remembered my dream early that morning. I went back to my journal and saw the note. "Cheetos, what are you doing here?" It was Cally telling me she was leaving and that John was there to help her. His laughter from the dream echoed in my mind. It was the same laughter he had when he was telling Cally and me that we were crazy. What an amazing gift she gave me in that message! I'm sure she didn't even know that I was there to receive it. But, there was joy in her voice.

The wake and funeral were later that week. There was no question that I would be attending. I had to be there, as did half the call center. I am thankful that the company I worked for figured out a way for individuals to attend. They were allowed to come to the funeral in the middle of the day. I was not paid for all the time off, but I didn't really care.

My friend, Wendy, came to the funeral. She did not want to go to the wake the night before because she did not want to see her friend, lifeless. I did not blame her. I did go to the wake. Cally was not there. The body she resided in while here was in a casket looking yellow. There was no evidence of Cally's light. She was gone. I imagined that she flew away on her angel wings, free from all the trials she endured on this earth. Yet, I knew she was not far. I knew she would want to be there for her "momma" and "sissy-la-la". She would be there with Matty, because she knew he was like her, too. She was very protective of her brother and sister. She cared deeply.

When we went into the church for the funeral, the casket was in the back of the church, open for review. People coming in to sit down had to pass the open casket. I was with Wendy and she was anxious about having to walk past the body to be seated. "I want to give Kathy a hug, but I can't look at Cally. I just can't do it!"

"Then, let's just sit and you can see Kathy afterward."

There were people there who asked me if Cally's biological father was there. I don't know why I knew he wasn't, as I had never met him. Cally had referred to him as a "sperm donor" for so long, I just assumed that he would not be there. Plus, I knew that he had disassociated from her, refusing to include Cally as part of his current family. He had daughters that did not seem to know that Cally existed. Though, Cally would go spend time with his mother, who was in a nursing home. She showed her enormous love and respect, going to visit with her regularly, even when the woman was outwardly mean to Cally. "She's my grandmother, regardless of what my Dad wants. He cannot change the fact that I am his daughter. And, she is old and just goes along with what he says. I continue to visit her, regardless of his actions to keep me from being a part of his family."

During the service, I thought about what a beautiful person my friend was. I wondered if he would ever regret not knowing her. I wondered what kind of karma he was creating with his failure to recognize this beautiful, caring, light for so many. This daughter that touched so many lives with love and respect. She had a great dad in Terry. In fact, when she spoke of her "dad," I always knew she was talking about Terry. As I sat there, I wondered what price her biological father would pay in this lifetime for doing such wrong to this Divine golden light. I actually felt pity for him. He would never have the chance to reconcile his wrong.

At some point, months after the funeral, I did ask Kathy about the "sperm donor". She confirmed that he did not show up at the funeral, but said she had talked to him, or his mother. It came down to him using some lame excuse for not coming. Regardless, he made a million decisions to not be a part of Cally's life and would not be part of her death either. This was just another choice. It always comes down to decisions.

After the funeral, weeks went by until Cally's spirit came to visit me. I was working on something in the clinic and smelled flowers. It was a combination of roses and peonies- sweet and pink. I looked up to see her standing there, smiling at me. "Hello!" I said, surprised at her sudden appearance.

"You can see me?"

"Yes."

"Cheetos told me that you could see me, but I didn't know you had advanced so far!" she said. Then, twirling around in a circle, she said, "So? How do I look?"

She had this beautiful pink glow around her that sparkled with flecks of what I could only describe as bluish stardust. When she twirled, I could smell the flowers again. "Beautiful! You have no yellow to your skin! You are beautifully pink and full of color and life." One of the things I had come to understand was that spirit was more alive than some breathing humans on this planet.

"Ahhh! Thank you!" she said.

"How are things?" I asked her. "Did your life review go okay?"

"Yeah," she said, "it wasn't as hard as I thought it would be. Though, I didn't know about all the things I contracted for this last go around."

"So, there is an actual contract?" I asked.

"Oh yes!" she nodded as she said it.

"Should I be worried?" I wondered aloud.

"Well, no," she hesitated, "But, you will anyway."

"I suppose you are right there." I was a worrier. "I am trying to trust my guidance."

"You are doing great!"

"Hey, you owe me money!" I laughed, as I said it. "Now, how am I going to collect it? I don't know where you live, or work, anymore!"

With a laugh, she said, "You are so funny! You don't even care about the money." Her smile did not change. She just smiled.

"I'm not ready to come there to collect it." I went on.

"Oh, I know. You've got a lot to do yet."

"Shit! I was hoping that wasn't the case!"

"Don't worry," Cally said again. "We won't let you do it alone. We can't leave you."

"It just feels like I am alone." I felt her hug me and kiss me on the cheek, as she often did when she was alive. It was like being enveloped in the love of the entire world, warm and overwhelmingly beautiful, but fluttery and light.

"Trust me when I tell you that my debt is paid."

"I'm not worried about that, it was paid before you left." Which debt were we talking about? Was she referring to her debt to me, or her debt to her Creator?

She understood what I meant and brushed it aside. Then, she asked me, "Can you do some things for me?"

What could I possibly do for her? She could be everywhere at once. She could help others just by being asked. I didn't say anything out loud, as I knew it didn't matter. She knew exactly what I was thinking. She just sighed a little and continued talking, as if I had already agreed. "I need you to take my client files and deal with them."

"Yeah, I can do that," I told her.

"I have to thank you for talking to Sonya about the stuff." I had spoken to her roommate, Sonya the day after Cally died. Cally's family would be going to Cally's apartment to collect her things and her cat, Nala. I had asked Sonya to pull Cally's journals, which contained her secrets.

"It's not my story to tell and I don't think it needs to be told."

"Thank you."

"Cally, I am worried about Jenny, Matty and your mom."

"I know. The drinking and depression," she confirmed. "But, unfortunately, I cannot step in here. This is part of their path. I love them and I work with their angels to help when I can. But, I cannot appear to them how they want me to appear."

"You are in a better place than here, right?" I asked, hopeful.

"Oh yes! It is beautiful! Do you remember?" she asked the question like I should.

"No." I admitted.

"Do you remember that vision you had of the farmhouse with the little girl running around the kitchen?"

"Yes."

"The reason why you had that vision was because you were there. You were part of it."

"Past life?"

"Yes. You will have more visions of past lives. I will be in a lot of them. So will John."

"I have such a hard time believing in past lives, even though I have seen them," I admitted.

"You'll get over it." With a laugh, she just waved that away, too. "I have one more request and I need to go."

When I nodded, understanding that she was expanding, she said, "There will be grace in this. When you write your first book, I want you to write about grace."

"Okay?" I questioned it, not really understanding. Was she talking about the blessings that come from death?

"I know you don't understand now. Your first book will not be done for a few years. When it is done, you will remember things out of order. You will remember conversations with spirit that you have never spoken to others about, but you will remember the conversations as you write. When it is done, you will understand. Just remember to write about grace."

"I will write it down in my journal when I get home, so I don't forget."

"Do that! Write down 'Cally wants me to remember Grace.' You won't forget." She smiled at me with such radiance that I knew I would not see her like this again. I wasn't even sure I would see her spirit again. "I wish you understood how loved you are. Remember, nothing you do will ever change that. You are loved by many spirits here!"

As I watched, she shimmered once and seemingly flew up through the ceiling. I saw the sky above her, as if the ceiling opened. It was filled with golden light. Cally's pink glow mixed into the gold with her stardust flecks and she was gone. I was staring at the ceiling in the warehouse of the clinic.

Upon returning to my apartment that afternoon, I went to my journal and started writing about grace. As I did not know exactly what I was supposed to write, I looked up some definitions of the word. The definitions that were given to me by Google were "1. a refinement of movement or simple elegance. 2. (in Christian belief) the free and unmerited favor of God, as manifested in the salvation of sinners and the bestowal of blessings. 3. do honor or credit to (someone or something) by one's presence." So, was I supposed to write about how God graced me with the gift to discern spirit? Or, was I supposed to write about how spirits grace us with their presence? Although I could see the gracefulness, poise and elegance of angels, I was pretty sure this was not what she was talking about, as Cally and John were as klutzy as I was. This was all written in my journal from May of 2010.

After that day, I saw Cally only a few more times. She would come to me in my dreams. On occasion, she showed up when her friends were on my table receiving massage. Yet, within a year and a half, I felt she had transcended or split. I would get the same floral smell I identified with her, but I would not see her, or hear her. It was like only part of her was there.

As I wrote this part of the story, I realized Cally was right. I never told anyone about this conversation with her. I did write it in my journal, so when I recalled the conversation while writing, I could refer back to my notes. I did not remember the conversation with her until I started writing this chapter of the book. Plus, she knew that when I recalled the conversation and my notes, I would know exactly what she wanted me to write. She did not want me to write about the word and what it meant. She was giving me a clue. She was telling me to write about the person named Grace. She was telling me to write about her niece, Grace, who had not yet been conceived. At the time I recalled all of this, Grace was 5- years-old.

Chapter 20

Finding Grace

Figuring out that grace was actually a human with that name gave me this sense of wonder. When I went back to my journal and saw what I had written that day in May of 2010, there were many clues from spirit.   I read through the entries, hungry to see what else was there that I had forgotten. At some point, I quit journaling on a regular basis. I don't know if it was because my guidance was coming to me in different ways, or if I just lost interest in writing my feelings, ideas and happenings of day-to-day in a book. Having recalled information from five years ago and verifying it in my journal made me think that there have been many messages I have forgotten, or missed.

So, what was the reason Cally told me about Grace before she was even conceived? Why did her visits change, where I could no longer see her? Was it so that I could believe that our Spirit never dies? Was she telling me that she was coming back in Grace? Plus, how did she know? I was not unfamiliar with reincarnation, as I had seen some of my past lives. If she came back in Grace, how was her spirit still presenting to me in other ways? I could feel her and smell the flowers when she was there, even when I couldn't see her.

Sometimes, we need to see to believe. Like doubting Thomas, we have to probe the wounds to make a decision to believe. At other times, we accept a situation as truth, and do not question whether it is true, or not. With most instances involving spirit, I have made the choice to trust whatever my intuition was telling me. Although my intuition told me it was not a bunch of crap to dry and use fertilizer, I was not going to put total belief into reincarnation either. One thing I believed beyond everything else was that our spirit never dies. Therefore, I had to trust that it went somewhere. Why would it not come back into life somehow?

When I began to look at reincarnation, I had to look at science. Physics taught me that we are all made of matter. Our bodies are composed of carbon, oxygen, water, and many other elements that I do not remember from chemistry, biology or anatomy. But, it was my religious beliefs and pursuits that introduced spirit to me. Spirit became matter by entwining itself with a body of element, yet was not bound to the physical body. My guidance confirmed this.

Some may have referred to this sudden understanding of Spirit as an awakening. For that year and a half, I was awakening to Spirit in a way I never thought was possible. It broadened my gift so much that new things began to surface for me. Slowly, my senses began to open to many different forms of communicating with many different things. I smelled color. I saw all forms of Spirit- some of it was not of a higher purpose. I understood why my cat thought he was a prince. There were dreams about people and events that were in another place and time. Yet, they were not dreams, but memories manifesting in my dreams. I'd touch someone and know things that I did not want to know. I'd stare at the wall and get a movie clip of a different scene running in front of me. I'd hear foreign languages and understand what was being said.

The entries in my journal described some of the things that were happening. Yet, I did not remember those things until I went back to my journal while writing my story. In retrospect, it was probably the writing in the journal which allowed me to forget the experiences. I was experiencing so much that I had to write it down in order to sleep. If I didn't, I would stay up most of the night in conversation with Spirit. One night, I even felt like I was flying with angels. When I woke up exhausted, I wrote this in my journal. I looked up to find my guardian angel, Timothy, standing there. He told me that I had been traveling with them.

When I finally asked about Grace being a reincarnation of Cally, my guides said, "You are only partly correct."

"What part?" I asked, perplexed.

"There is one body, many parts." It was Archangel Uriel talking to me. While studying the angels, I found out that Uriel in Hebrew meant *fire of God,* or *one who is like God.*

When Uriel did not explain further, I asked, "So, is that true with Spirit? There is one Spirit, many parts?"

"There are different kinds of spiritual gifts, but the same spirit. There are different workings but the same God who produces all of them in everyone."

"Where have I heard this? Have I heard this before?" I questioned out loud.

"Of course you have, Dear," John said, "throughout many, many lifetimes."

"No," I shook my head. "This is Bible material."

"It is also in other religious texts that are non-Christian, but of the same God," John said. Then, he laughed and said, "You could ask Bill where to find it."

"Why don't you just tell me?" I asked him.

"She got you there, Johnny." This time, it was my father, using John's familiar nickname. "Look in your Bible, Toni Marie. It is 1 Corinthians 12."

"That is not the only reference, but it is the one you recognize," Uriel said.

We talked into the night about the Spirit being part of the "grace of God" and what it meant. I read more passages from my Bible and became more convinced that Spirit was our

272

universal Divinity. It belonged to not one body, but many. This Divinity belonged to all religions, not just the Christian faiths. It belonged to all forms. Our bodies came from matter, but our Spirit came from Source. Due to the fact that Spirit was from the same Source, I came to the conclusion that we were all of the same Spirit.

In my notes, I even asked about Satan and the demonic spirits that I had seen. "Are these lower level energies also from Source?"

"Yes."

"But, how does that fit into Source?" I asked.

"That is where free will comes in," Michael explained. "You choose to work for the highest good, or you don't. We do not see it as good or bad. We see it as it serves the good of all, or not. We cannot intervene in your decisions. It is not for any of us to judge, either. If we were to judge, we would be judging ourselves."

"I am still confused," I said. "Is Cally now Grace or not? And, is that even what she meant when she told me to write about Grace?"

It felt like there was a collective sigh among the angels and other Spirit in the room. Maybe the concept was too difficult for me to grasp in the middle of the night? Or, maybe I was making it harder than it was supposed to be? I knew that I had the ability to make the simplest answers so convolutedly complex that even I could not understand it.

Archangels Michael and Uriel looked at each other, as if willing the other to try again. Michael shrugged a little and Uriel just shook his head. "Let's start with grace." It was Uriel who lost the staring contest. "It is by grace that we are. Even the Buddhists recognize the statement 'I am' is a Divination of Source, and many Christians discredit the spirituality of a Buddhist. So, by the Grace of God you are. Do you follow?"

"I think so. I am Divine by the Grace of God."

"Yes. But, that Grace is all encompassing. It gives you the gifts you have and those gifts are also the Grace of God."

"Okaaaay…"

"Those gifts are not entrusted to one person. Everyone has access to the same gifts."

"I totally agree! I have been saying that all along!" I said it excitedly. Everyone in the room nodded.

He seemed to think a minute before he said, "There is grace in death, too, which you already know. Everything has grace, even things that are perceived as bad. It serves a purpose. It is by grace that we have the ability to choose our own path. That does not go away. All spirit continually evolves and makes choices by grace."

"So grace is fluid, ever changing and of many parts?"

"Exactly!"

Parts of the last year clicked into place, like puzzle pieces. When I hit my head, I had a choice to live or die. I had a choice to embrace my gifts, or repress them again. Every day, I had choices in my life that moved me in and out of contentment. Some days, it was easier to face challenges than others. But, I continued, regardless of it being hard or not.

John made a choice to go, rather than live a life dependent on me. In his decision, he went back to Source. It was through Grace that he was helped me. I would not have started working with Spirit at all if it had not been for John coming to me. I would have continued to hide, insisting my own sanity was questionable. There was Grace in all of it.

Uriel could hear my thinking and was coming in through my writing. I was very tired, but knew there was more he had to say. When I looked up, he said, "So, Grace does have the spirit of Cally in her, by the grace of God. Though, might I add, she also has your spirit, and that of her blood line, as it all comes from one spirit. But, what you know as Cally will not be the same in Grace. You will know it comes from her, as the similarities will present. Plus, you understand spirit at a different level than most because of the gifts you have accepted and learned."

"So, spirit does reincarnate?" I persisted.

"Yes. But, it takes on different aspects of itself."

"And this is part of grace?"

"It is one of many parts of grace."

In reviewing my journal, I knew I must of drifted off somewhere in the middle of the discussion of the Grace of God, as the information in the journal was vague. In fact, I think that most of the conversation happened in a dream, which was recorded in three quick blurbs- "grace of God, reincarnation true, one spirit." Regardless, I did not recall most of the discussion until I sat down to write this part of the story. I probably wrote what I did in the journal so that I could go to sleep and forget about it.

As I have already discovered that I could not have come into my intuition with such clarity without experiencing the loss of my spouse, I knew that losing my friend also had a gift. It would have been so easy for me to look at all the grief and loss and assume that was all that was there for me. I had seen many individuals become less than who they were after the death of a loved one. Unknowingly, I decided that I would not become less than myself because I was being called to become more than I was. I made a choice to use the gifts I was given to help others. By helping others, I am helping myself.

Without my head injury, I could not have been open to seeing Spirit. I had repressed that gift from childhood because of the fear of how I would be received as a medium. I would not have been able to deal with John's death in a clear, calm way. I could not have the gift of spirit without the head injury, as I would have rejected it. I could not have one without the other.

When John died, he gave me a gift. He came to show me and tell me that what I was seeing was real. He told me that I was not crazy. Then, he warned me that I would receive more spirit. If he had lived, I know that he would not have been the same man that I married. I would not have been free to explore my gifts because every day would be occupied with burden. He chose to go and I did not have to make hard decisions to remove life support, find alternative care and resources to care for him, and any number of other medical concerns. I am grateful that I had time in this life with him. I am grateful that he did not have to suffer, living a life he would have hated. I could not have such an understanding of my gift without his instruction from the other side. I could not have one without the other.

As I began introducing my "angel readings" into my bodywork practice, I accepted that more gifts would start surfacing. In turn, there would be more individuals that would look at what I did and find fault. Without the help of the spiritual world, I would not have understood what my highest good looked like and that I did not need to have concern for judgment coming from others. Without the guidance from spirit, I would not have faith in myself, my higher power, or the highest good of everyone.

I started to look at all the things that could not come without the other. Without rain or light, there would be no rainbows. How would we define evil without first knowing what is good? If I was never lonely, I would not understand the importance of reaching out to others. Without poverty, I would have never seen the abundance in my life. There are gifts in everything. You cannot have one without the other. There can be no life without death. Would there be Heaven without Earth? Would there be salvation without grace?

I have been blessed. Many times, I have been blessed. The blessings would never have come without everything else. It all came down to a decision. I decided to have one, knowing that it came from the other.

www.ingramcontent.com/pod-product-compliance
Lightning Source LLC
Chambersburg PA
CBHW060253100426
42742CB00011B/1739